CHURCHILL'S UNEXPECTED GUESTS

CHURCHILL'S UNEXPECTED GUESTS

Prisoners of War in Britain in World War II

SOPHIE JACKSON

First published 2010

The History Press
The Mill, Brimscombe Port
Stroud, Gloucestershire, GL5 2QG
www.thehistorypress.co.uk

British Library Cataloguing in Publication Data.
A catalogue record for this book is available from the British Library.

ISBN 978 0 7524 5565 5

Typesetting and origination by The History Press
Printed in Great Britain
Manufacturing managed by Jellyfish Print Solutions Ltd

CONTENTS

one

WHEN THE FIGHTING WAS DONE

GENEVA CONVENTION

Any discussion on prisoners of the Second World War needs to begin with an understanding of the Geneva Convention, the twentieth-century document that formed the basis for how prisoners in Britain and to a degree in Germany were confined. Its limitations, however, opened it up for abuse and despite many prisoners believing it to be a legal document that must be upheld by their captors, it was in fact only a moral code. None of the rules laid out in the document had to be followed, only considered and interpreted as the captors saw fit.

For German troops in particular, the fact that the British and Americans upheld the Geneva Convention made being captured by them a far better option than being captured by the Russians, who had no intention of treating Nazi prisoners well. As part of the agreement, both Britain and America had to make provisions for a neutral country to visit the prisoners to ensure their well-being. Russia, on the other hand, could hide away their prisoners, abuse them and leave them to die without any other nation observing them.

The very first Convention had come about in the nineteenth century after the publication of *A Memory of Solferino*, written by Henry Dunant, a Swiss man who had helped tend to dying and wounded soldiers for three days and three nights after the battle of Solferino in 1859. The fight between the French and Austrians left 6,000 dead and 40,000 wounded. The French army's medical teams were overwhelmed; they had more veterinarians than doctors. The harrowing aftermath of the battle that Henry Dunant recorded in his book inspired Europe to create some form of document that would protect those wounded in battle.

The first meeting to discuss the Convention occurred in 1864, when sixteen nations came together in Switzerland and twelve agreed to sign the first Geneva Convention and created the Red Cross flag (a reversed version of the Swiss flag).

One of the most significant factors of the treaty was that it established the neutral status of military medical personnel. Further treaties discussed at the peace conferences held at The Hague were established before the Great War, and during that conflict, neutral countries such as Switzerland took informal responsibility for ensuring prisoners of war were treated well. This included visiting camps and hearing prisoners' complaints.

However, the main provision of the Convention was to deal with wounded soldiers and this left deficiencies in the guidelines for the treatment of captured prisoners. In 1929 the nations came together again and signed the second version of the Convention. Included in those nations that agreed to follow the Convention was Japan. The Soviet Union, due to spending the 1920s isolated from the international community, never signed the treaty.

This proved disastrous for German soldiers captured by the Russians; they were starved, brutalised and often left to die in the freezing Eastern European winters. For Russians in German camps the situation was little better as the Germans decided to ignore the Convention in relation to their Eastern European prisoners, while following it in regards to their British, French and American prisoners.

The Convention set out a number of points that a 'hostile government' should follow in relation to its captives, including:

They [POWs] shall at all times be humanely treated and protected, particularly against acts of violence, from insults and from public curiosity. Measures of reprisal against them are forbidden.

No pressure shall be exercised on prisoners to obtain information regarding the situation in their armed forces or their country. Prisoners who refuse to reply may not be threatened, insulted, or exposed to unpleasantness or disadvantages of any kind whatsoever.

Their identity tokens, badges of rank, decorations and articles of value may not be taken from prisoners.

Belligerents are required to notify each other of all captures of prisoners as soon as possible ...

Work done by prisoners of war shall have no direct connection with the operations of the war. In particular, it is forbidden to employ prisoners in the manufacture or transport of arms or munitions of any kind, or on the transport of material destined for combatant units.[1]

Much of a nation's compliance with the regulations was due to reciprocity. Britain held strictly to the Convention, even after the war ended, in relation to its German prisoners for fear that if they did not something untoward might happen to British prisoners in German hands.

But like all agreements, the way the rules were interpreted and followed depended on individual camp conditions and their commandants. Britain also found it difficult to treat its prisoners equally in all its dominions, and its camps in France and Belgium were particularly notorious. In addition, the government struggled to gain uniformity between British and American camps, some German POWs having been sent to the United States.

The German prisoners themselves tended to see the Geneva Convention as a law that could be enforced by the ICRC (International Committee of the Red Cross) and punishments were imposed for infringements. In truth, the Convention had no standing in international law; the regulations were principles which the nations that had signed were only morally obliged to hold to.

For the most part, sticking to the Convention's principles as rigidly as Britain did was due less to national conscience than to the real fear of reprisals against British POWs. An early example of how reprisals could grow and cause international and national concern happened in October 1942.

On 7 October the German High Command announced that it would be chaining the hands of all British soldiers captured in Dieppe because 'British troops had tied the hands of German soldiers in the raids on Dieppe and Sark'.[2]

The British government's response was to declare that if British soldiers were not freed from their chains by 10 October, an equal number of German prisoners would be shackled. The German High Command immediately replied by ordering that three times the number of British prisoners should be placed in chains. They refused to release the men until Britain agreed that never again would they tie the hands of Germans captured in raids.

The Swiss government, trying to act as a neutral mediator, attempted to break the deadlock of 'German reprisals and British counter-reprisals'. They appealed to the nations involved:

In conviction [sic] that it was with reluctance that Germany, as with Britain and Canada, was led to shackle prisoners of war, Switzerland, the protecting power for German interests in the British Empire and for British interests in Germany, has suggested simultaneously to the interested governments a date on which those prisoners should be freed from their shackles.[3]

Earlier on the day that the Swiss gave their appeal, the Prime Minister had been questioned on the subject, particularly about whether Canada had been consulted before German prisoners in their country were ordered to be shackled by the British. He responded: 'On account of urgency it was not possible to consult any of the Dominion governments upon the counter-measures to the German shacklings which were deemed necessary in October by the government.'[4]

After the appeal, the Foreign Office announced that all German prisoners in British hands would be unshackled as of 12 December 1942. The Canadians issued a similar statement that German prisoners would be untied without delay. This did not have the desired effect in Germany, where British POWs remained shackled until December 1943.

The official reports compiled after the war noted that it was not just the tying of German hands that had caused reprisals, but the discovery of a number of German bodies riddled with bullets lying at the bottom of the cliffs at Dieppe. In the end, it was not diplomacy that ended the stalemate but a shortage of camp guards, who became slack in the shackling of their British prisoners. The prisoners' hands were meant to be tied in the morning and untied at night, but eventually the guards merely gave the shackles to the POWs and ordered them to tie their own hands. Though punishments were still inflicted for failing to wear the chains, very often the camp staff simply ignored the infringements.[5]

Prisoner Nationalities

For the most part, when people recall the POWs held in Britain during the war they usually remember them as either Italian or German. Indeed, most official documents would give the impression that only men from these two nations were ever captured. Yet the range of nationalities of the men held in the UK was in fact far greater than that. In 1947 8,000 Ukrainian prisoners of war were brought to Britain from Italy. Once here volunteers were selected for agricultural work and for long-term residency in the UK.[6]

The Germans had conscripted a number of soldiers from their neighbouring countries along with any they conquered. During one interrogation the seaman being questioned revealed he came from Vienna in Austria, but considered himself a German. He had been a labour conscript sent to Germany in 1939 and from there he was eventually drafted into a U-boat school at Wilhelmshaven.

As the war progressed, the Germans made a habit of encouraging their prisoners to join the military. Another POW who found himself housed in a camp in Suffolk was Czechoslovakian and had been effectively press-ganged into the German army.

In the latter stages of the conflict the Germans even tried to persuade British POWs to re-enlist under the Nazi flag. Similar tactics were used on Russian prisoners to greater effect.

Russia and Germany were bitter enemies; the Nazi regime viewed the Russians as little better than savage animals. German soldiers feared capture by the Russians knowing the horrors they would endure, and the situation was no better for any Russian who fell into Nazi hands.

British POWs were often held in camps next door to Russian prisoners with little more than a barbed-wire fence separating them. Yet the conditions either side of the wire could not have been more different. While the Germans followed the Geneva Convention in regards to their British captives, they saw no reason to treat the Russian enemy similarly. The Russians were starved and brutalised. If any tried to escape they were shot immediately. There are stories of British POWs feeling so sorry for the starving Russians that they would try to throw some of their rations to them, but when a Russian attempted to retrieve the food they were shot dead by a guard.

Unsurprisingly, when faced with such horrors and knowing that their leader, Stalin, had effectively washed his hands of any man who was captured – considering them lost in action – the Russians were prepared to accept the Nazi offer to join the German army.

To the British, the nationality of their prisoners was not as great a concern as their political attitudes. German prisoners in particular were classified and housed according to their beliefs. Prisoners were screened upon entering Britain and then placed into one of four groups: Grade A (white) were considered anti-Nazi; Grade B (grey) had less clear feelings and were considered not as reliable as the 'whites'; Grade C (black) had probable Nazi leanings; Grade C+ (also black) were deemed ardent Nazis. 'Blacks' were usually housed in special camps, often situated in remote areas where escape was harder.

Grading was essential not only for security, but also prisoner welfare. While most camps had a mixture of 'white', 'grey' and 'black', some camps were predominate in one grade of prisoners. On occasion a Grade A (white) prisoner was placed into a Grade C+ (black) camp; in such situations the results were often assaults on the 'white' anti-Nazi, occasionally with fatal consequences.

Grade C+ were not supposed to leave base camps and they were not to join working parties except under the supervision of the Director of Labour. If a C+ prisoner was discovered to have been accidentally sent to a working camp then he was to be immediately transferred away.

German Deserters

It is sometimes easy to forget that not all German soldiers believed in Hitler and the Nazi regime or wanted to fight Britain. Some made active attempts to be captured and then reveal useful information to the British; there were even those who, after being taken prisoner, asked to join the British army.

One such man was Uffz Franke, who had spent a year in a German prison from March 1941 after 'expressing views prejudicial to the regime'. Despite his anti-Nazi feelings he was sent with a Panzer division to Africa in 1942 where he arranged to be captured by the British. Franke had anti-German feelings and when flown back to the UK he applied to join the British army. The authorities considered using him as a stool pigeon, a line of work that required a good deal of courage as the risks if exposed could prove fatal. Franke was turned down for the role as he was considered 'lifeless and timid'.

Deserters, however, were not always the most reliable of sources for information. Many were keen rather than useful and had gathered information randomly, usually without understanding the context, to try and be helpful to their captors. The interrogation services regularly double-checked information and reported its accuracy, often with disappointing results.

The 'Diseased' Italians

Among the earliest POWs to arrive in Britain were large numbers of Italians; many had been captured in the Near East where they were all too willing to surrender to the British troops. Once they were captured it was necessary to set up camps in Britain and transport the new captives there.

Amid the many concerns about finding a suitable location for a prison camp, one was primary in certain people's minds. The Italians were being shipped from a location rife with disease, many were already suffering from some form of illness, and it was vital to the War Office to protect the health of the British public.

In a letter written by Dr P.G. Stock on 17 June 1941, he reports:

> From the information in his possession Brig. Richardson anticipated that malaria, dysentery, typhoid fever and pediculosis had been rife amongst the prisoners. He said that the army authorities would provide the necessary hospital accommodation at the transit camps and would see that the men were disinfected: in addition he was considering having them all inoculated against typhoid fever, but feared that a number might be carriers of malaria, dysentery and typhoid.[7]

Three thousand Italians were due to arrive on 8 July of that year, the first of a proposed 50,000 Italian prisoners that were being shipped to Britain in the hope that many could help fill the labour shortage in the country. Suddenly the authorities were gripped with unexpected panic. They had sick men heading their way carrying potentially lethal diseases to an unsuspecting population.

The men were to be initially housed at two transit camps, one in Lodge Moor, Sheffield, the other in Prees Heath, Shropshire, but where the men were to go next was still in debate. A telegram was forwarded to the Ministry of Health discussing the problem.

In a letter dated 24 June 1941 it was stated:

> The Minister [of Health] apprehends that certain infectious diseases may be prevalent amongst these Italian Prisoners of War and is anxious that all possible steps are taken to prevent any spread of such diseases … the minister is particularly concerned to ensure that precautions are taken in districts to which these prisoners of war may be sent to work as labourers … I am to add that the risk of the spread of malaria is greater in some parts of the country than others, and the ministry would be prepared to furnish you with information on this point if it is agreed that steps would then be taken to avoid … sending any Italian prisoners of war who may be carriers of malaria to a district where there is the most risk of spreading the disease.[8]

Eventually a list of the locations for the Italian POW camps was announced:

> The Labour Camps for the first 3,000 Italian prisoners of war (for Agriculture) due to arrive about the 8th July, 1941, are located as follows:-
> (a) Farncombe Down. 1 mile east of Baydon, Wilts.
> (b) Melton Mowbray (Leicestershire).
> (c) Ledbury. ¾ mile south (Herefordshire).
> (d) Doddington. 4 miles south of March (Cambridge).
> (e) Rugby. 2 ½ miles south (Warwickshire).
> (f) Anglesea. Glan Morfa. 3 miles south of Llangefni.
> (g) Baldock-Royston area. (Hertfordshire).[9]

Almost immediately concerns were raised about the choice of certain locations. Even with health screening at the transit camps, involving the taking of in-depth medical histories and giving inoculations, there was still a fear that a disease-carrier might be unintentionally sent to the wrong location. The greatest fear was the spread of malaria which is contracted from the bite of an infected mosquito. If a mosquito were to bite an Italian who was a carrier of malaria, it would then drink infected blood and potentially pass this on to anyone living in the vicinity.

Further reports of the potential dangers were hastily drawn up. Dr P.G. Stock wrote:

> Anopheline mosquitoes are found throughout England and Wales, but fortunately our experience shows that it is only one species, namely Anopheles Maculipennis, which is concerned in the spread of malaria. Moreover, it is only one variety of this species which is the real danger … (variety Atroparvus). This variety is only found in sufficient numbers to constitute a real danger … along the south coast of England, east of Wareham in Dorset and up the east coast as far north as the River Humber. Included in this area is the valley and the estuary of the Thames, the Isle of Grain, the Isle of Sheppey and places such as Harwich, Dovercourt, Walton-on-the-Naze, Ipswich, Great Yarmouth and the country bordering the Wash, namely parts of Norfolk, the Isle of Ely and Lincolnshire.
>
> … From the War Office letter of the 28th June, it is noted that a certain number of Italian prisoners of war are to be sent to Doddington, four miles south of March in the Isle of Ely, and unless these men can be diverted elsewhere special precautions should be taken in the district. The matter is

of importance as we are now in the most dangerous period of the year for the spread of malaria.

This news provoked consternation among the concerned parties and, writing to a Mr Shute of the Malaria Laboratory, Horton hospital, Epsom, Dr P.G. Stock was determined to clarify the risks: 'The War Office, however, want to know how far inland from the coast the danger zone exists. I believe most of the coastal belt is a reserved area for war purposes and the question does arise whether the area reserved for war purposes is sufficient for malaria purposes.'[10]

Mr Shute's response was tinged with the difficulty of the situation:

> I would suggest that the War Office be told that the danger zone is <u>anywhere in England where stagnant water is brackish.</u>
>
> We cannot give any hard and fast rules about this because in some areas brackish water may extend some miles inland, while in others it may not exist for more than perhaps a few hundred yards inland.

Yet the War Office still felt that the urgent need for agricultural labourers in the east outweighed the risks of malaria. In another letter it was suggested 'that prisoners from Lybia born north of the River Po and apparently free from malaria may be sent to Doddington'.

By now it was 10 July and the situation was becoming urgent. It was arranged that Mr Shute, along with a Dr Banks, would inspect the camp location and conditions and report back. But as the same letter summed up forlornly:

> I don't know that there is anything that can be done except for the Medical Officer of Health to keep a general surveillance on the prisoners in case any of them show signs of infectious disease … If in spite of the care taken to select them there is any case of malaria, great care should be taken that it is removed as soon as possible and I think you better let me know at once.

It was 22 July when Mr Shute penned an urgent report to Dr Stock on the situation:

> I met Dr Banks at Cambridge on Monday July 21st. We visited two proposed sites …

<u>The Doddington Site</u>
At one end of the field which had been selected, there is a large marsh.
<u>Anopheles Maculipennis</u> are numerous and adults are plentiful in the farm
buildings close to the field.
<u>The Ely Site</u>
There is a swamp on the proposed site and <u>A. Maculipennis</u> are equally
numerous here.
<u>Comment</u>
<u>Anopheles</u> are very numerous in both these areas and breeding is taking
place <u>in the fields where it is proposed to erect the camps.</u>
Both sites are potentially dangerous.
It is too late in the season to clear up the proposed site. Even if anti-larval
operations were carried out at once it would not be satisfactory because
adults are so very numerous and most of them will live on for the remainder of the summer.

Scrawled in heavy black ink at the bottom of the letter, Stock added his
own thoughts: 'the proposed site does not seem to be at all suitable.'

When Dr Banks wrote his report he pointed out even more reasons,
aside from mosquitoes, why the site was unfit for a camp:

The site [at Doddington] which was small and low-lying, looked liable to
flooding in winter time, but no-one was able to confirm this. The only
definite proposal for essential services already considered was the supply of
main water from the Town and no arrangement had been made for sewage
disposal. From the nature of the land it did not appear likely that satisfactory arrangements could be made for this, especially when … the possible
presence of enteric carriers required extra care in this connection.

I had had in mind a number of other possible objections to a camp of
this kind in the Isle of Ely, namely lack of hospital provisions, particularly isolation, lack of essential services, etc. but it was not necessary to
discuss these.

The combined reports were damning. Shute believed that any site located
in Ely would be dangerously close to mosquito grounds, while Banks felt
the areas were too isolated and rural to provide suitable living quarters.

In the end, however, the War Office decided that the risks of malaria
should not outweigh the need for a camp in the Ely area. The camp location was changed from Doddington to 'Old Militia Field' Ely. This did
not go down well with everyone; writing to Dr Banks, Dr Goodman of

the Ministry of Health was appalled and astonished at the way the malaria risk was seemingly being ignored.

But the decision was made and Goodman received a letter notifying him that the prisoners would be arriving at the camp from 23 August. The Ministry of Health still hoped that they might be able to get permission from the military authorities so that Mr Shute could go down and take 'blood films' from the prisoners and test it for malaria. Mr Shute wrote:

> It is to be hoped that the local doctors [at Ely] will at once notify any cases of fever in the village (especially children) where the cause of the fever presents any difficulties. I wonder if the military would be prepared to spray with 'flit' the animal houses in the farm close to the site. If they would do this in October, just after Maculipennis have gone into hibernation, and again in March, just before they come out again, the adult population would be much reduced next summer, at least for two or three months before migratory swarms appear.

There were perhaps some who considered their fears slightly exaggerated. Writing on 11 September 1941, Lieutenant-Colonel Sandiford stated:

> You will be interested to know that of 1,454 Italian prisoners of war received at 17 camp, Prees Heath Shropshire, on 6th September, 1941, 42 were recovered para-typhoid cases treated at Durban, South Africa, and of 1,000 prisoners of war received at 16 camp, Lodge Moor, Sheffield, on 9th September, 1941, 33 are similar cases.
>
> As you know, a careful history of each man is taken and those with a history of enteric or dysentery infection are examined to ensure they are not 'carriers' before allowing them to proceed to their various labour camps.

Mr Shute took blood films in September from the prisoners and wrote to Dr Roxburgh, the lieutenant in charge of Old Militia Field labour camp, with his initial findings on 28 October:

> I have not yet finished examining all the films of the prisoners … But I thought you may like to know that we have examined a hundred (thick and thin) and that so far no Plasmodia have been found.
>
> As you know, between relapses, parasites are very rarely found in the peripheral blood and therefore a parasite free blood is not evidence that the person has not had malaria, or that he will not relapse in the future.

I mention this because if any of them develop fever which is not readily accounted for, you may like to have a blood film examined for parasites.

Mr Shute was also asked in December 1941 to draw up a map of England and Wales showing the areas where malaria was likely to be a risk. By January thoughts were returning to 'preventing mosquito breeding and it was proposed that notices be sent to the camps outlining how to stop mosquitoes breeding in the static water tanks.

At last the procedures for ensuring prisoners did not bring disease to England were formalised in March 1942. All prisoners had to be inoculated against enteric bacteria in South Africa. A brief medical history of each prisoner was to be prepared by the Italian medical officers during the voyage to England. The men were expected to have been cleansed of vermin in South Africa, but routine disinfestation was to be performed in the ports where the men arrived. In the case of typhus, however, it was expected that each POW would be given a careful examination when they arrived at their camp and a 'Serbia barrel' would be set up to bathe men with suspected infestation. Night soil was to be incinerated and any cases of minor illness would be dealt with at the camp. Anything more serious would be treated at the nearest military hospital or EMS hospital.

Ely was not alone in attracting malaria concerns. At the camp at Horsham, Sussex, which already contained Italian prisoners, a ditch was discovered to contain breeding mosquitoes and Dr Hope Gill, who was in charge of the medical side of the camp, was put on alert that should any suspected malaria cases arise, blood films should be taken at once.

It was not only in the east where camps had to be reconsidered. The proposed Melton Mowbray and Rugby camps were already being replaced by proposed camps in Garrendon Park, Loughborough, and Fenny Compton, Warwick, as the Shute and Banks reports on Ely were being read. Only a week later the War Office changed its mind again – there would be no camp at Fenny Compton and instead one would be set up at Ettington Park, 4 miles north of Shipston-on-Stour. In fact, it seems the various authorities were getting quite muddled with their camp locations. A hasty memo from the Ministry of Health read: 'We have been in touch with Wiltshire as regards the Farncombe Down camp ((a) on your list) and have been informed that Farncombe Down is in Berkshire, just over the border from Wiltshire.'[11]

However, one site in the east did meet with approval. Shute wrote of the Royston site in Hertfordshire: 'This appears to be an ideal site and there are no mosquito breeding grounds in the area. It is waste ground very dry and chalky.'

There remained anxiety about the spreading of disease; in particular, the disposal of sewage from the camp caused consternation. Concerns were raised about the disposal of urine, though 'it may be possible to sterilize the urine by bleach before allowing it to discharge into a soakpit'.[12]

A PRISONER'S INSIGHT

When renowned German theologian Jurgen Moltmann published his autobiography, it included a chapter on his experiences as a boy serving in the German army and ending up as a British captive. German accounts of their time as prisoners in Britain are few and far between; the account in *A Broad Place* gives a great insight into the experiences, living conditions and attitudes of the prisoners.[13]

Jurgen Moltmann was only in his teens when he was called up in July 1944 and found himself a German soldier rather than a student of mathematics as he had intended. He spent much of his first days at the barracks learning to drill, dismantle and assemble machine guns, and how to identify different ranks within the German army. Despite almost being sent to the front for further training in August of that year, it was not until September, after the British had launched Operation Market Garden, that he found himself heading for battle.

First travelling by train in a cattle truck, then marching 35km and encountering scattered soldiers retreating from the fighting, some wounded, Moltmann's unit eventually arrived at the Albert Canal and dug themselves in. That night they came under heavy fire for two solid hours; Moltmann, lying in his dugout, managed to fall asleep only to be woken by his corporal shouting 'out and back'. Confused and alarmed, the men followed the corporal into nearby woods, finally running through to the village of Asten; there they heard grenades whistling overhead all night and falling into the village. Distantly they could hear the sounds of fighting on the canal bridge.

The men became lost; with no one apparently in command they drifted about trying to re-form their unit. By morning those who had survived the night came together. Only half their number was left; any man sleeping close to the canal bridge during the onslaught had been killed. With British tanks rumbling in the distance, the young men dispersed across the fields and made their escape in the dead of night.

Later, they learned their commanding officer had taken refuge in a cellar in Asten waiting to surrender to the British.

Near escapes were to become a pattern of Moltmann's short army career. During the remainder of 1944, until February 1945, he served in Holland before participating in the Battle of Venrai. Moltmann recalled taking shelter in a farmhouse with several other soldiers; they were in the midst of the British and while hiding heard a swathe of tanks rumbling towards them. At the last moment the tanks turned away, much to the men's relief. Moltmann peered through the glass in the building's door to see what was happening and to his surprise saw British soldiers looking back.

The Germans ran out the back door with sub-machine gun fire at their backs, through a pigsty and behind a haystack. That night they crept past the village that was now occupied by the British, lit by the flames of burning haystacks.

Moltmann was later part of a reconnaissance troop sent out to scout the enemy. They came across no one until they hit an open path; there a Red Cross ambulance had struck a mine. The two British drivers lay on the road dead. The troop carried on and eventually came across a knocked-out English tank perched on a small hill. Being close to the British lines, they hid behind it and listened for a while, but came away with no information.

With their territory under pressure from the British, the German forces found themselves pushed further and further back. In January Moltmann was once again sent out on reconnaissance work, this time to see which nearby villages had been occupied by the British. Wearing snow-shirts and rubber boots, and led by a soldier named Fritz Goers, the troop crossed a river in rubber dinghies and walked to the nearest village. At first it seemed peaceful; they searched a few houses but found nothing so walked further down the main road. Suddenly a flare attached to a mast went off and the men dived for cover in a field. Gunshots rang out from the houses and rained down on them until Goers called out in English that he was wounded and needed help. The shooting stopped and in the darkness Moltmann and another man crept away and back to their unit.

Moltmann's experiences of war were not just the constant struggle to avoid being captured by the British, but also the day-to-day deprivations and miseries that stuck with him. For six months Moltmann never slept in a bed, only in a dugout; if he was fortunate, on dry straw. When military reinforcements joined them from the east they brought with them lice which were impossible to get rid of. The German delousing stations could do little better than offer the men a shower and clean their uniforms. So the men sat in their trenches and 'cracked' lice.

Moltmann began to suffer from boils on his neck. The medical order-lies attempted to cure them by painting on a tincture, but to little effect, so Moltmann spent most of his time wearing a gauze bandage.

In February 1945, with the British getting ever closer, Moltmann's unit marched to the village of Cleves. Coming under heavy fire, they fled to a hill where an observation tower stood and parachutists were awaiting orders. They were still under fire and shot blindly into the dark. As the night wore on, a unit of British tanks roared up the hill and occupied the tower. Moltmann and his colleagues now realised they were hemmed in.

When morning came it was discovered that most of the officers and parachutists had already decamped, leaving the ordinary soldiers to fend for themselves. They formed small groups and attempted to break through the British lines. Moltmann's unit only succeeded in reaching a field in front of the hill where a cemetery stood. The British began firing on them from all sides and several men fell. Others put up their hands to surrender. Moltmann and a few others made a dash for a semi-ruined house nearby and hid inside.

As the firing grew fiercer the other men threw their rifles out of the windows to show they were prepared to surrender. Moltmann slipped up to the attic of the house and found a sheet of iron to hide under. The British entered the house and shouted for the Germans; Moltmann remained under the sheet of iron and managed to stay undiscovered. As night fell he slipped from his hiding spot to see if he could escape, but only went as far as the cemetery because the road beyond, which he would have to cross, was far too busy with British traffic.

Returning to the ruins, he searched the property hoping for something to eat or drink. Finding nothing, he went up to a room beneath the roof and lay there in the dark. The next day he watched the British advance into the Reichswald Forest from the window in the roof.

Moltmann knew he had few options remaining; if he did not escape that night he would have to surrender. He was tired, hungry, thirsty and crawling with lice, all things that depleted his resolve to stay undetected by the British. That night, however, he did manage to cross the cemetery and the road beyond; he found himself between abandoned tanks and started to make for the front once more.

Again, Moltmann's journey was fraught with near misses when he came close to stumbling on British soldiers. While walking through woodland he saw the British approaching and lost his glasses leaping into a bush for cover. Later he trudged through a British communications line where everyone was asleep in their tents and never knew of his presence. But things were now getting bleak for Moltmann; he was on the brink of exhaustion, his only sustenance being snow water from puddles.

While searching for a place to hide in a dense part of the woods he was surprised by a British soldier. Moltmann shouted, 'I surrender'. But the soldier mistook him for one of his mates messing around. He called other men over and they began to talk to Moltmann, realising he was one lone German.

Moltmann was uncertain of what would happen to him, but the men treated him well and the following morning their lieutenant gave him a mess tin of baked beans. It was the first food Moltmann had tasted in days.

Later he was taken to the assembly point for prisoners. The British there were armed with DDT sprays for delousing the new captives. When sprayed under the clothes the DDT quickly dealt with the lice, survivors crawling out of the men's collars and cuffs. For the first time in many weeks Moltmann felt the relief of being free of the terrible pests.

It was 15 February 1945 and with mixed feelings Moltmann now began his life as a POW. He was first transferred to camp 2226, Zedelgem, near Ostend. No longer faced with death and the struggle to survive, the prisoners found themselves confronted with a new problem. Becoming prisoners gave them a chance to think and dwell on what had happened and what the future held. Despair engulfed many, some even fell sick because of it; for those from East Prussia and Silesia the future looked bleak. Their homelands were now occupied by the Russians, the natives driven from their homes. These men had nothing left and no idea of what they were going to do.

For others the thing that tormented them most was the memories of lost comrades. In the heat of battle death had to be swept aside as you leapt from conflict to conflict; in the camps there was time to think. Many men were suffering from 'survivor's guilt', wondering why they had survived and their comrades had not. Many too were suffering from post-traumatic stress syndrome, a condition unrecognised at the time but which led many into a spiralling state of depression and despair.

Moltmann was one of these men. At night he suffered horrific dreams when he saw the faces of the dead and would wake in a cold sweat. He felt alone, his hopes and dreams for his future dashed and, like so many of the men, was struggling to come to terms with what might lie ahead.

The Belgian POW camp held its own horrors. The men slept in huts on three-tier bare wood bunks; there was scarcely any other furniture and the bunks had to double as seating. At night the huts were locked, the only sanitation coming in the form of two buckets. It was after dark when the horror really began. Many of the prisoners were former Hitler Youth leaders or SS men, and when the hut doors were locked they went after anyone who was critical about Hitler, the Nazi party or Germany's chances of arriving victorious at the end of the war. The screams of men being beaten up echoed through the huts.

Moltmann shared a bunk with an engineer from Augsburg, an older man no longer subject to the reckless heroism of youth. He would not allow Moltmann to go to the aid of any of the attacked men, knowing the savagery of the assailants. He would hold him forcibly down in his bunk if necessary to prevent him getting involved.

Moltmann had sunk into the grips of depression. The boils that had constantly plagued him in the trenches now spread across his body, but he did not care to do anything about them. Eventually it was the Augsburg engineer who once again looked out for him and escorted him to the medical orderlies. Moltmann's condition was severe enough for him to be sent to a hospital in Ostend. There he was able to take a bath and, with fresh clothes and a decent bed, he slowly healed, finally returning to the camp scarred but well a fortnight later.

The end of the war brought new problems for the prisoners. The Red Cross in Belgium declared that, as there was no longer a Germany, they were not responsible for the prisoners anymore and abandoned the camp. Left in the care of the Belgian authorities the prisoners found their rations cut, and the British porridge they had become accustomed to eating in the mornings was watered down.

From time to time people were taken out of the camp to work. On one such occasion Moltmann was in a work party pushing a goods truck when he came upon a blossoming cherry tree. Struck by its beauty and brilliance, he stopped to admire the tree and it was at this point that the depression in him began to lift and he started to come alive again.

During the summer of 1945 groups of prisoners began to be sent home; Moltmann, however, was never among them. Camp life was tedious and boring, so he joined a choir and pretended to sing to pass the time, but most of his daily life was employed waiting and hoping that the next call would be for him to go home.

In August Moltmann was summoned along with others to get onto a transport at Ostend. Finally, expecting to be travelling home to Germany, they boarded the ship. The next morning when they went on deck they were shocked to see Tower Bridge. They had arrived in London.

The prisoners were taken to Hampton Park where they were searched for watches or valuables, before being sent on another journey up north, finally arriving twenty-four hours later at a camp in Ayrshire, Scotland. This was camp 22, Kilmarnock.

While not his home, the British camp was far better than its predecessor in Belgium. The Nissen huts only held twenty men each and they slept on individual beds with straw palliasses. In the centre of the hut stood an iron stove to provide warmth.

At Kilmarnock the men's mental well-being was taken into more consideration and the site included a recreation ground, a library, a POW orchestra, a canteen and a chapel; an attempt was also made to stimulate the men's minds with lectures and talks. Moltmann often sat with other prisoners listening to a Catholic professor of philosophy talk about the ideas of Aristotle and Aquinas.

Despite this the camp could still feel claustrophobic and Moltmann regularly volunteered for work outside the camps. His favourite role was as an electrician in a NAAFI camp where he only had to follow a skilled workman about, move light cables and mend electric irons. He also had a friend in the camp who stored away tins from damaged boxes. He often gave Moltmann a tin of corned beef or sardines which the German would discreetly eat in the lavatory.

There was plenty of work to be done in post-war Scotland, so Moltmann fulfilled many roles. At Dumfries House he cleaned parquet flooring, at a Scottish mine he dug coal and at a cement factory he came away covered in grey dust. At New Cunnock, a German working party dug sewage trenches for the laying of pipes for a new housing estate. Moltmann was among them performing the back-breaking task of digging through partially frozen earth, while another team worked on creating the roads for the estate.

The work teams were always hungry from their intensive labour and Moltmann regularly approached the Scottish or Irish overseers asking for bread. This became such a common occurrence that soon Moltmann had become the interpreter for the work gangs and no longer had to work himself. Instead he acted as a go-between for prisoners in the camps who were constructing toys and the Scottish families who were happy to buy them and provide the Germans with a small income.

During his time in Scotland Moltmann became friendly with a local family named Steele; they called him Goerrie and treated him as a friend. When he appeared one day with a runny nose because he had no handkerchief, Mrs Steele gave him a new packet of hankies to keep. She also sent uncensored letters from him to Hamburg – a charitable act that could have got her into a lot of trouble with the authorities.

In fact, the Scottish families of Kilmarnock on the whole treated the prisoners with hospitality and kindness. Their friendliness to former enemies made many Germans feel ashamed, but at the same time it brought them out of their isolation and reminded them what it was to be human and part of a community.

In March 1945 Moltmann's mother was told he was missing, which for many families meant their loved one was dead. It was not until August that Mrs Moltmann was put out of her misery when someone came to see her and said he had seen her son in the Belgian POW camp. Around September Moltmann was allowed to send his first postcard home to let his mother know he was all right; limited to twenty-five words, his message had to be short and simple. Not long afterwards he received his first letter and learnt with relief that all his family were alive and that his father was a POW in France.

It was also in September that prisoners were confronted with the images of concentration camps in Belsen and Buchenwald. Photographs displaying piles of dead bodies were pinned up in the huts. Some called it propaganda, others said it was justified for the destruction of German cities. But for many it opened their eyes to what had really been happening and what the Nazi ideal truly stood for. The shock of realising what had been done in the name of their country, of what they had fought to continue, filled many with bitterness and anger. Some never wanted to return to Germany again; they disowned their country and chose to stay in Britain.

For Moltmann any patriotic feelings he had once had were destroyed. He may never have returned to Germany had not his father's Jewish friend returned to Hamburg at the end of 1945. If that man could see past the brutality and return home, Moltmann felt he should be able to as well. But that could not change the feelings of shame and guilt that many Germans felt and continued to feel long after the war was over.

There was one experience in the camp that was to change the course of Moltmann's life. One day a chaplain came to camp, gave a short talk and distributed Bibles; for many it was a mundane event, but for Moltmann it led him in a whole new direction. Lost and consumed by German guilt and shame, he worked slowly through the Bible each night coming to identify with Jesus and his sufferings, and eventually Christianity became his lifeline and his lifelong calling.

By early 1946 Moltmann realised his captivity was not going to be over any time soon. Britain needed a workforce and the German POWs could in part alleviate this need, therefore repatriation began with those unable to work. Many men attempted to prove they were unfit for work in any way possible, showing old scars as evidence of their disability. Moltmann, though lacking suitable scars, attempted to fake illness by drinking an excessive amount of coffee to give himself palpitations. This failed to convince his captors that he should be returned home swiftly.

Moltmann was not as desperate as some of the men to return home, so instead he applied to go to an educational camp in England where he could repeat his German final school-leaving exam, the *Abitur*, which was necessary to enable him to go to university back in Germany. The possibility of retaking this in England was extremely good news for those who had had their studies disrupted by the war; once again these men could contemplate and feel excited about their future prospects.

Having passed an English language test, Moltmann was put on a train under armed escort and taken to camp 174, Cuckney, Nottinghamshire. The camp was set in the picturesque grounds of the park belonging to the Duke of Portland and was established as a school for trainee teachers and Protestant pastors destined to work in post-war Germany. It had been founded by the YMCA but financed by an American businessman, and it clearly made an impact on Moltmann, who considered it a generous gift from the British to their German prisoners.

At the entrance to the school Moltmann was met by high-ranking German army chaplains who, prior to arriving at the camp, he never even knew existed. The camp was split between trainee teachers, theology students and, in the middle, those working towards their *Abitur*. The lessons were run by German teachers and the final result was recognised by the Hamburg educational authorities.

Living accommodation consisted of Nissen huts arranged among oak trees around a hill, upon which stood the camp chapel. Taller Nissen huts set aside for teaching and eating were set behind the sports field near the parade ground.

For the inmates of the camp it felt as though they had stepped into some form of monastic institution set away from the world. Their day began at 6.30 a.m. and ended at 10.30 p.m. During that time, instead of the bored frustration of the ordinary camps, they were able to feed their minds, not least by visiting the YMCA library which was well stocked with a range of books. There were novels, both American and British, as well as books on theology, philosophy, mathematics and much more. The YMCA also produced specialist books on German topics, particularly discussing the effects of dictatorship and the origins of the war. For the prisoners who had for so long been starved of intellectual fodder it was an exciting and stimulating experience, and many like Moltmann read as much as they could.

At the end of 1946 Moltmann passed his *Abitur* and was officially classed as a student within the camp. He had at first contemplated joining the trainee teachers, but his recent experiences and interest in the Bible led him to join the theology students to train as a pastor. The camp welcomed many distinguished German and British theologians who gave lectures to the students and Moltmann was absorbed. He attended his first ever church sermons. Life at the camp had unexpectedly opened up a wealth of new possibilities for him. In Moltmann's own words: 'We received what we had not deserved, and lived from a spiritual abundance we had not expected.'

He even, along with several other POWs, attended an SCM conference in 1947. Dressed still in their wartime uniforms, the prisoners were apprehensive of the reception they would receive and what questions might be asked of them about the horrors of the war. But they were welcomed with open arms by the other Christians who were attending the conference. They were even approached by a group of Dutch students who spoke of the Gestapo horrors, Jewish arrests and ruined towns of their homeland, but who wanted to extend a bridge of Christian feeling to the prisoners and be reconciled with them. Afterwards they all embraced.

Moltmann finally left England in 1948 on the second to last transport from the camp. His experiences of war had been harrowing, but his time as a prisoner had opened his eyes, brought him back to life and even given him a new focus. His life was to be changed forever and though his story was only one of thousands, it gives an insight into what it was like to be a German prisoner in British hands.

Notes

1 International Committee of the Red Cross: www.icrc.org/IHL.NSF/ FULL/305?OpenDocument.
2 *The Times*, Wednesday 9 December 1942.
3 Ibid.
4 Ibid.
5 Report on Stalag viii B, Lamsdorf, concerning ill-treatment and reprisals against British and Canadian POWs. The National Archives, Kew. WO 311/86.

6 Home Office Circular No 170/1948 – Release of Ukrainian Prisoners of War for Civilian Employment. The National Archives, Kew.

7 Medical inspection and selection of camp site for Italian POWs. The National Archives, Kew. MH 55/1884.

8 Ibid.

9 Ibid.

10 Ibid.

11 Ibid.

12 Letter from Lieutenant-Colonel H.A. Sandiford, Director General Army Medical Services. The National Archives, Kew. MH 55/1884.

13 Jurgen Moltmann, *A Broad Place: An Autobiography*, SCM Press, 2007.

two

THE GERMAN GUIDE BOOK

INTERROGATION

The large numbers of prisoners being brought to England required some system to assess and interview them for any useful war information. This responsibility fell to the Combined Services Detailed Interrogation Centre (CSDIC) in London, as well as other centres on the Continent. The quality of the information varied both in its accuracy and its usefulness. Some prisoners, especially those who were conscripted from conquered nations by the Germans, were all too eager to pass on information, but this was often of limited use. Others proved harder to interview and the British developed a variety of techniques to uncover military secrets.

The CSDIC kept detailed reports of their interrogations and also any relevant opinions on their interviewees. Most questioning revolved around military equipment, tactics or organisation, but revealing information could be obtained by listening to prisoners' opinions on their commanding officers, morale, the progress of the war and even on Hitler.

On 18 November 1941 two Germans, Leutnant Kiefer and Feldwebel Risch were captured in Egypt. They were subsequently sent to Britain where the CSDIC had the opportunity to interrogate them. Kiefer and Risch worked within the Abwehr, the German military intelligence and counter-intelligence organisation. They were asked numerous questions about their involvement, including details about the other personnel who were there. The transcribed responses provide simple and in some cases mildly derogatory descriptions of their fellow Germans and give an insight into the lives of these men before the war.

Among the men mentioned were Aigner, a Feldwebel (sergeant) badly injured in a crash, and the man Leutnant Kiefer replaced. There was Major

Arnold who worked from office 1016 and was described as 'rather bald, and looks a soldier'. Then there was Astor, a Berliner responsible for radio propaganda, but said not to be a party member; perhaps that explains the sarcastic description the men gave of him: 'dark and wearing glasses, he looks what he was, a Bank director.'

Another man, Blaum, was depicted as 'very clever and somewhat nervy'. He had a double doctorate, but was not considered pro-Nazi in his sympathies. Risch told of Major von Eschwege, who he had to report to on arriving from Berlin. Eschwege had been an author prior to the war and had spent three months in America. Unsurprisingly, he was responsible for the text of pamphlets used in the 'unsuccessful Calais enterprise'. A German named Kappe had also spent time in America working on films before the war. He had taken part in the French campaign and wore the golden party badge, but 'was always in financial difficulties, was far too stout for his age (28), and drank far too much'. Another called Segelke had been with Risch on a failed mission to Calais; he was 'thin and gawky with an egg-shaped bald head. Very unsoldierly appearance.' While a man named Speiss, whose present whereabouts neither man knew, was an anti-Nazi who regularly complained about being overworked, but was also a 'first-rate tennis player'.[1]

The interview also revealed personal grudges that were carefully recorded, such as that between two Germans named Schoneich and Bohle. Schoneich had been a schoolmaster but was banned from working in schools due to a disagreement with Bohle, so now worked on French propaganda. The Abwehr also included Germans from different countries, including a Viennese, a Swedish and a Palestinian German, while others had connections with different nations, such as Scheuermann who was married to a Dutch woman and an unnamed Swede who had been a police captain in Turkey during the last war and had been recruited for the Abwehr.

Aside from learning information about the people involved in the war, the CSDIC were eager to learn as much as they could about German weapons and machinery. When Obergefreiter Kurt Bachmann and Leutnant Karl-Friedrich Jenning, members of the German air force, were captured in Tunisia on 12 December 1942, one of the things they were questioned on was Tiger tanks.

Bachmann had been in the workshops where the Tiger tanks were being put together, though he stated that the lighting had been poor so he could not answer on points of finer detail. He described the hull as 8m long and when he had stood on a packing case hard against the tank's side the turret was about 70cm from him. This enabled British intelligence to estimate that the tank's width was 3.4m.

Bachmann had sat inside the tank and had been able to witness how the turret moved. He was able to draw detailed sketches of the vehicle for his captors. He described how five or more men could sit inside and how the W/T operator sitting at the rear would have his wireless set attached to the bulkhead wall. Other details that Bachmann revealed caused consternation or perhaps disbelief among the British.

'P/W alleges that there are six machine guns (!) in this tank,' one portion of the report stated, while further on: 'P/W claims to have heard that the armour thickness of the front plate is 35cm (!).'

Other information that drew an exclamation mark from the interrogation team was on the tank crew's performance: 'P/W states ... that the gun has to be loaded from below ... and talks of loading by hand at the rate of 24 rounds a minute (!).'[2]

From Bachmann's description the Tiger tank was shaping up into a formidable weapon in the military arsenal. Aside from its turret and alleged six machine guns, he talked of a mortar mounted on the side. He also described how the only means the driver had of seeing out was through a periscope, which the British were sceptical of. Through further questioning they discovered this was an assumption on Bachmann's part, though he had seen 'a whole case full of various kinds of mirrors' which appears to have fuelled his ideas of periscopes.

More interesting still to the British was what Bachmann could tell them about the damage a British gun had made to the tank. Bachmann explained that the tank had been hit at short range by a British shell, possibly from a 12cm (60-pounder) gun. He described the hole in the tank 'or rather dent' and even made a plasticine model for his interrogators' benefit. Bachmann gave clear details of the dimension of the dent and the condition of the metal on the tank's side, though he did complain that he could not properly show the sharp edges of the hole using plasticine.

Bachmann was clearly happy to provide such useful intelligence to the British. This perhaps seems surprising until further information in the interrogation files reveals some soldiers' attitudes to their commanding officers. In one particularly bitter report a former German air force lieutenant talks of officer selection: 'One was an old party member, that was all he had to recommend him. He used to clean the streets at home and couldn't write a letter.'

Later on, talking about reinforcements for his signals personnel, the same POW said: 'There are nitwits out there who cannot even transmit a single letter. They have changed people so much – they sent me technical people from depot battalions who could handle bombs, or form infantry or supply columns – but no signallers. I should think all our signallers have been killed in Russia!' And then returning to his pet subject of officer advancement: 'In the Air Force things have been tightened up [1942]. In 1939/1940 it was the men you wanted to get rid of who became officers – the ones who gave trouble.'

A corporal, one of the GAF ground staff, added his voice to the discontent: 'There is a rule that any man in the [Reich] Labour Service who has served twelve years in the army and has risen to sergeant may apply for a commission ... Far too many of them were made Lieutenants. They are absolute fools.'

One final comment on the subject came from a major who worked with anti-aircraft units: 'The Predictor[3] calls for the co-operation of thirteen men who must not let themselves be distracted by anything ... Yet for this job they pick the worst men – the deaf, the blind and the mentally deficient! And for the guns too.'[4]

However, the British interrogators observed that the only two AA gunners they had met were comparable in ability and experience to British soldiers in similar employment. They also commented that many men praised their commanding officers, 'though an occasional [officer] may be inclined to conceit and arbitrariness when they first come from their officers' schools'.

Yet they did state that German officers on wartime commissions did not have to go through selection tests but were chosen based on their efficiency reports during active service.

The British were intrigued by the German selection process and asked more questions. They discovered that officers were selected in 'special psychological centres' where the men would spend a couple of days working through various tests. They even identified the possible locations of the centres where the large and permanent test apparatuses were kept.

Simpler tests such as 'a few sums, an essay, etc.' were carried out at training units when the men enlisted. One applicant for a commission was even tested in the field while on the Polish campaign and the 'selection board [on which no psychologist figured] met there and then to turn him down'.

The selection process itself could begin when the man was as young as 17; parents or a guardian would write on the man's behalf and submit evidence of 'nationality and birth, Aryan descent, and educational standard'. The candidate then had to show they had command of the German tongue and was required to write an essay detailing their personal history from infancy to the present day. The essay needed to include details of any involvement in Nazi youth groups, sporting proficiency, hobbies or any travelling the person had done.

Candidates would eventually be taken for psychological testing by the *Seelenspione*, 'Soul-Spies', which was how the men commonly referred to the psychologists. The tests themselves were intriguing and designed to assess the man's mental attitudes and make-up.

First he was ushered into a waiting room with chairs ranging from comfortable armchairs to hard backless stools. A range of reading material was laid out on a table, from philosophical and scientific journals, to comics and pornographic magazines. Most informants explained to the British that they had quickly guessed that this was the first test and that they were being filmed. This was the case and the psychologists were monitoring the men for signs of restlessness, laziness and lack of interest, among other things.

The men had to then write another essay on an abstract subject such as love, honour, blood or war. They had fifteen minutes to complete the task and the test was 'enlivened' by sudden changes in the room's lighting and the dropping of weights from the ceiling.

Yet another essay was the third test. The candidate was shown a series of postcards and asked to pick one as the subject. He then had twenty minutes to complete it. Next he had to give an address to his companions on any subject, examples being 'matches' or 'underclothes'. The address could be humorous and light-hearted.

With the mental tests out of the way, endurance tests began. One involved the candidate being loaded with a 25lb pack, being told a complicated message and then forced to climb wall bars until the point of exhaustion. He then had to repeat the message.

Another test required the candidate to walk across a beam high over the ground and tie a rope to a number of hooks. A plank then had to be put in position so the man could cross to another beam.

Finally there was a meeting with one of the *Seelenspione*, which was designed to be an informal chat on many topics with an embarrassing question suddenly addressed to the candidate 'to test our shockability'. During the talk a gramophone would be playing classical or romantic music. The British interrogators noted that this was part of the test: 'The candidate is encouraged to let his fancy roam and to say what image or colour the music suggests. Woe to him if he does! For to be so aesthetically and sensitively-minded is not compatible with officer status.'[5]

Understanding the German military psyche and the way officers were selected would be vital to the British and to their POWs. When plans for re-education commenced near the end of the war, misunderstandings of the psychology of the German prisoners could prove extremely detrimental to the programme. The British struggled through most of the war to truly understand their enemy, just as the German POWs often failed to comprehend why the British behaved the way they did towards them. Interrogation was only one part of generating a mental map of the Nazi foe.

Aside from the general testing, the candidates had to undergo specific tests applied to men in particular units. Flying personnel had comprehensive medical examinations of their eyes, nose, sinus passages, ears and teeth. They were tested on their ability to write and complete sums when the air pressure of the room was gradually dropping. They had to finish the test when they realised they were losing self-control and had to write out that they had remembered to 'dive and straighten his machine' before it ended. Again, psychologists and medical personnel were assessing the men at all times.

A further test had the candidate strapped into a chair that rotated vertically and horizontally. While the chair was rotated into different positions he had to perform mental arithmetic and at the same time control a lever in each hand that he had to move in relation to coloured light signals. Later he had to perform the same test while blindfolded and had to state the number of times he had been rotated.

A mechanical test required candidates to put together certain objects, such as a bicycle pump or plug, in a limited time.

One of the candidates who explained these tests to the British was a German NCO. He had been a pilot for nearly three years and was the son of an army officer, yet had failed to receive his commission. The pilot excused this with the fact that he had refused promotion because he did not want to miss out on any fighting. But the British interrogator noted in his report: 'It may be, however, that he created the same impression on his superiors as he did on the writer: a rather moody, eccentric, slap-dash fellow, adventurous, "flying-mad", boastful and intolerant of discipline. He had shown marked instability in choosing a job.'[6]

U-BOAT CREWS AND THE ENIGMA MACHINE

The earliest prisoners to arrive in Britain were U-boat crews and they were the lucky ones as the majority of German submarines sank with all hands lost. For the British these men were a vital source of information. British shipping routes were in severe danger from the German navy, putting supply and personnel convoys at risk every time a ship left port. Learning all they could from the U-boat crews was one way to potentially save British ships from destruction.

On 16 January 1940 the crew of U35 were questioned. Prior to being captured U35 had been patrolling between the Scottish and Norwegian coasts in appalling weather conditions. They gave the British a prime opportunity to understand submarine tactics, including the fact that the U-boats always submerged when they saw a plane without bothering to attempt to identify it, that they used Morse code or flag signals to communicate with their base and that in any future attempt to sail into the Atlantic the U-boats would not travel via the Dover Straits. Instead the plan was for U-boats to sail as far north as possible.

But of the greatest interest to the British was the Enigma machine. The Enigma was a cipher machine the Germans used to encode their communications. Originally on sale commercially in the 1920s, the German military realised its potential and used a more complicated version to encrypt messages. The machine employed sets of 'wheels' that could be used in billions of combinations to encode ordinary messages. Only by understanding the way the wheels were arranged when the message was encrypted could the ciphers be cracked.

The Germans considered the machine foolproof and all their U-boats carried them. However, through interrogation reports, the help of Polish mathematicians, who had brought an Enigma machine from Germany before the outbreak of war, and the intensive work of British code-breakers at Bletchley Park, the Enigma machine was finally cracked. This not only gave the British a clear advantage by enabling them to intercept and decipher German communications, but some historians argue that it also shortened the war by two years.

This, of course, all took time. So it was no wonder that when U-boat crews were captured they were comprehensively questioned on the elusive Enigma machine. But German crewmen were not liable to give up information to direct interrogation. When Lieutenant Pennell had to interview a member of U35, Funkmaat May, he adopted the stance that the British were already using the Enigma machine on their own submarines and acted as though he just wanted to compare the British and German models. Over successive interviews he became friendly with May and was able to gradually learn more and more about the German cipher machine.

May explained how the 'wheels' of the machine were numbered and changed roughly every two days by an officer. He also provided a drawing showing the layout and another quick sketch of one of the plugs used as a connector. Pennell continued to encourage May in his belief that the British were using an Enigma machine but that it was 'very slow'. May remarked their machines were extremely fast and then helpfully drew a diagram showing how messages were encoded.

Pennell persisted in stating that he felt the machine would be of little use for sending immediate operational signals as the receivers would not be able to distinguish this message as being more urgent than ordinary communications. This prompted May to reveal a vital piece of information. He explained that a specific signal, which his interrogator believed to be in Morse code, was sent out before an Enigma message to inform the receiver that it was an 'immediate operational signal'.[7]

Not all prisoners were so easy to obtain information from; some were more elusive. Telegraphist Ernst Felbeck of U15 told his interrogators a subject was 'secret' when he didn't want to answer a question, and when pushed his answers became evasive or misleading. When asked about beacon frequencies that Felbeck used for direction finding he refused to answer, explaining they were 'very secret'. While Felbeck was stationed on U15, the submarine had been chased and attacked with depth charges on more than one occasion by British ships.

Felbeck was not alone in his caution; another seaman who was interviewed also refused to answer questions when he considered the information secret. But even elusiveness led the British to information, and when the seaman was asked if the 'I. I.' signal indicated a weather report and did not deny it, his interrogator judged that to mean the answer was affirmative.[8]

HEROES AND VILLAINS – SECRETS OF THE INTERROGATION FILES

Among the details of military tactics, armaments and weapons the British interrogators uncovered other snippets of information that they duly recorded. Some of the stories they heard held no real relevance to the war itself but were so fascinating that they wrote them down anyway. Others revealed the real horrors of the conflict. A man might be reticent with his interrogators not through any desire to protect German secrets but to conceal his own. Silence could be the sign of a guilty conscience.

Such seemed to be the case with a German POW named Lieutenant Corporal Theophil Brill, as his interrogator recorded: 'Brill at first attempted to be secure, possibly as a result of an uneasy conscience (he had participated in certain atrocities …), but finally broke down.'[9]

Brill had been involved in operations in Croatia and Slavonia against the partisans. On 24 February 1944 a German captain, Kinzler, was shot by partisans at his house in Nerecisce. Martial law was declared. Not long after, on 7 March, twelve German soldiers were killed when the truck they were travelling in was ambushed. Patrols sent out to search for the men failed to reach the scene of the attack, possibly because they feared being killed themselves. Instead they circled the area calling out the names of the lost men and, when they received no replies, assumed their comrades were dead.

Following orders issued by a Captain Wiesner and Lieutenant Keisinger, the Germans, including Brill, took sixty men from the villages of Humac and Praznica and machine-gunned them. Subsequently, Brill explained, they returned to the villages and burned them to the ground.

Other stories displayed the camaraderie enemy soldiers could feel towards one another. Under the heading 'Gallantry Story'[10] in the interrogation reports is an anecdote about a pilot named Rott. Between 29 March and 1 April 1943 he was flying his Focke-Wulf 190 when he came upon and engaged a Spitfire 20 miles south-west of La Fauconnerie. As both were flying at altitudes of 4,000ft, neither had the advantage, and for ten minutes the two aircraft manoeuvred trying to get the other in their sights. By this point Rott was running low on fuel and growing concerned about his next move.

He presumed that the British pilot must be in a similar position as he imagined the aircraft had just returned from an operational mission. Therefore Rott decided to take a chance: he wagged his wings, an international flying sign meaning 'goodbye'. Much to his relief the Spitfire pilot responded with the same sign and the two aircraft broke from combat, the pilots saluting each other as they left.

Another flying story that the British recorded was the confirmation of the death of flying ace Tonne. The British noted him as 'a brilliant fighter-pilot' whose death resulted from over-confidence in his abilities. Tonne liked to perform stunts over the airfield when he returned from a successful flight. 'He would wag his wings to indicate a victory.' On the last occasion that he tried the stunt it seemed he pulled out of the dive too steeply, lost headway and crashed. Such was the end of one of Germany's greatest flying aces.

Secret Conversations

One interrogation tactic of the British was to hide microphones in the prisoners' cells and then have people listen in to their conversations. Some microphones were quickly discovered by the prisoners, but it was not uncommon for cells to have more than one hidden in them, so the loss of a single microphone was not a problem.

Recording the men's conversations gave added insight into the German mindset and opinions on the war. Among the German generals held captive at the interrogation centre, Cruewell and another man named Armin were unusual in that they remained optimistic about the war. Most senior officers had accepted that defeat was inevitable and in subsequent recorded conversations Cruewell and Armin talked about their disgust at the 'disloyalty' and 'defeatism' of their fellow officers. They even suggested that such men would be shot on returning to Germany. In particular they marked out a man named Thoma as being the chief defeatist and responsible for bringing about the disillusionment of the other men.

There had been trouble instigated by Cruewell over some statements Thoma had made to another man. He had become rather isolated, as had Cruewell and Armin, who most other POWs viewed as 'windbags'.

However, while the German officers mostly viewed the current war as a disaster with no hope of victory, they also retained thoughts that a future war may still happen, with Germany coming to dominate the world, though the German generals were careful to regularly explain to the British officers that they would share this domination with Great Britain. Thoma, in particular, had high hopes of Germany's ultimate recovery.

The British noted that Thoma's views in fact made him a greater patriot to Germany than those who remained fixed to the Nazi party, but Cruewell did not share this view. His anger had flared when Thoma told another man that the Nazis would 'get Germany smashed up so completely that she would not even have a framework on which to build, which she had in 1918'.[11]

Thoma was keen to tell the British officers, at any opportunity, of two main lines of propaganda that they should be using. Firstly, that Britain should lay down its war aims in regards to Germany, stating frontiers, etc., the whole to become a focus for a peace movement within Germany; and secondly, that the British should reach Berlin before the Russians at all costs to save them from Bolshevism.

Russia was a very relevant fear in the minds of the POWs and regularly filled their conversations as they speculated about the future. Many were coming to see the British and Americans as their only hope of sparing Germany from Russian domination. In extracts from another recorded conversation, two Oberstleutnants discussed their concerns:

> '[If only] England would realise that … the peace terms will be dictated to her in just the same way as to us.'
>
> 'England may see the danger at the last moment.'
>
> 'But as long as our army is intact the English, with us, would be in a position to march against the Russians. That's the last hope. If our army is smashed, then the English will never manage it.'[12]

HUMAN TORPEDOES – THE ATTACK ON ALGIERS

One of the more intriguing aspects of the war that the interrogation reports bring to light was the use by the Italians of men in miniature submarines as human torpedoes. A very dangerous and risky operation, the human torpedo teams consisted of one officer and one diver petty officer. They carried double warheads, each section holding 90–100kg of explosives. They also had two time fuses that could be regulated up to ten hours.

A further team of men consisting of an officer and nine ratings were equipped with five limpet mines each. This technique would later be used by the British. Human torpedo attacks were carried out by the *Squadre d'Assalto*, a branch made up of volunteers, the men being some of the finest swimmers in Italy. The assault teams mounted various attacks, but the work was dangerous and many men were killed. The British were not always able to find survivors to gather information from.

On 7 December the *Ambra* submarine with its cargo of human torpedoes was sent to Algiers to attack ships. Poor weather, however, prevented them from attacking and the men had to wait in the submarine.

At dusk on 11 December a patrol ship was spotted and the submarine crash-dived to 270ft before proceeding to a sounding of 30ft. The divers were released in groups of three through the escape chambers of the submarine, each group taking seven minutes to get out.

The human torpedoes were carried in containers that had to be flooded from the submarine's tanks before they could be launched; this took about an hour. Once successfully launched, the human torpedoes headed for their marks and later claimed during interrogation that they had attached all their warheads to the correct targets.

The limpet teams had greater problems; heavy currents meant it took them one and a half hours to cover the 1,000 yards to the ships they were assigned to target. One of the limpet operators, having released his mine, panicked and climbed onto the British ship he had just mined, immediately causing the alarm to be raised. On hearing the alarm the submarine headed back out to sea without bothering to collect any of the divers. The human torpedoes scuttled their ships and swam ashore to give themselves up. The men later felt their attack had failed due to one of the limpet operators losing his nerve and the general unfitness of the teams from having to wait in the sub for four days due to bad weather.

A similar attack had occurred at Gibraltar just as the *Ambra* was arriving in Algiers. The Italians were hoping to make more use of the Spanish subjects in Gibraltar, but only two of the three human torpedo teams on the submarine were able to launch during the assault. One team was subsequently killed and the other was captured. From this failure the British learned from its captives that using depth charges had been the key to their successful defence of British ships. Afterwards a suggestion was made that when future attacks were detected, depth charges at irregular intervals would be the way to prevent the operators using their explosives.

GERMAN ATTITUDES AND MORALE

Understanding the German military mind became an obsession among the British. Time and time again POWs were interviewed about the attitudes and moral views of the different military ranks, even going so far as to secretly record conversations among the prisoners. Compiling material they drew conclusions about the men in their custody.

The German officer ranks particularly intrigued them, being so different from any comparable British class. They were a diverse range of men who despite constant in-fighting and quarrelling were united by the same spirit and desire to achieve success for the glory of the Reich. They maintained a singular philosophy: admiration for success and strength, both that of men and of countries. They despised weakness and even used the same coarse phraseology in their language.

They maintained a strong sense of duty and sincere patriotism. To the British camp staff it appeared these men were genuinely appalled by the atrocities of the Nazis and took pride in the fact that two prominent generals had thrown up their commands as a result of news of war crimes.

They were generally considered good leaders of men with a strong sense of responsibility for the welfare of the men in their command. They also took the view that they were, as they had been for generations, 'the most influential body of men in Germany, representing one of the few cohesive traditions of leadership in the country'.[13]

Yet interrogation reports taken in the latter years of the war show that all was not well within the German ranks. Many of the men were disillusioned and 'war-weary'. They were quite prepared if the opportunity arose to give themselves up to either the British or Americans. 'Only iron discipline,' stated one POW, 'enforced by armed NCOs keeps the men together.'[14]

Other reports suggested that the ordinary soldiers felt wrongly penalised by their superiors:

On 15 Feb 44, 11 Coy [a German unit] made a formal complaint to the effect that they had been issued with NO cigarettes or spirit ration for the month, although the officers appeared to have plentiful supplies. The Coy Command's reply was to have the whole Coy paraded, and to threaten to have every tenth man shot if there were any repetition of the complaint.

Generally speaking, severe punishments were awarded for the most trifling of offences. One man received fourteen days in a detention camp for having put some personal belongings in his respirator bag.[15]

Men who were not of German origin but had been conscripted from their home countries often felt a deep resentment towards their Nazi masters. Conditions at home were harsh; the Germans were considered brutal and their treatment was felt to be unfair. One report outlined some of the grievances:

[In certain units] it was forbidden to write letters in any language other than German. This was a great hardship for the Poles, whose relatives were mostly unable to read or write German.

P/Ws from the Austrian Provinces spoke with deep hatred of the things that had been done to them.

In Styria (Austria) five farmers were hanged in Feb 44, after having been caught for the second time illegally slaughtering cattle.

P/W stated that there was a shortage of everything in his home district, but NO signs of starvation. Bread especially was so bad as to be almost uneatable. Food rationing, it was thought, was being carried out with exceptional severity in Austrian villages.

P/W said that feeling among the peasantry against their German masters was so strong that, given the opportunity, even the old men would be glad to take up arms against them.

A further report was compiled from the combined interrogations of twenty-two German soldiers from 264 Infantry Division:

> It [264 Division] is composed mostly of older men, most of whom are married with families, and recruited largely from the working classes. They are fairly mature and capable of judging for themselves. The military developments of the last few months have convinced most of these men that a German victory is no longer possible.
>
> Especially in Yugoslavia the fighting against the Partizans has been very difficult, and mountain warfare, with the Germans always carrying their heavy equipment, against an elusive enemy, has often proved beyond the capabilities [of the men]. This factor, together with the Germans' knowledge that they could never achieve a striking success against the Partizans, has produced a general feeling of depression. In spite of several successful engagements with the Partizans the Germans found themselves coming up against more and more ... smaller bands. After nearly three years of fighting against guerilla bands (during which time the enemy was more than once eliminated on paper), a feeling of apathy was induced by the continual revival of resistance.[16]

For these men German defeat seemed inevitable; some feared that Russia would invade and control Germany and all able men would be sent to Siberia or devastated Russian zones for hard labour. They told their interrogators that they actually hoped for a British victory soon and that England might occupy Germany first. Their fears about the Russians would, unfortunately, not prove entirely unfounded.

Concerns about Germany's future were something that occupied the minds of most POWs. Their homeland was a country in disarray and many could not see the way forward. Later attempts by the British and Americans in re-educating the prisoners were to try and show them a positive way forward, but everyone knew that the process would be arduous. Rumours spread through the camps like wildfire, sometimes contradictory, but always circulating around fears for the future. Some POWs lived in the hope that the Russians would be too preoccupied with rebuilding their own beleaguered country to pay any attention to Germany, while others felt that the British would not allow Germans to be forced into hard labour by their Eastern European neighbours when there was so much work to do in Germany. Still others longed for Britain to occupy Germany and remain there until a liberal and democratic system of government could be established without interference. This was a hope mainly voiced by older men who could remember a country prior to the Nazi party and had not been influenced by the Hitler Youth.

There was even a rumour circulating that Germany would make a separate peace with England and that German Ambassador Ribbentrop was already in London to discuss the terms.

Notes

1 Combined Services Interrogation Reports. The National Archives, Kew. WO 208/3582.
2 Ibid.
3 The Predictor was a mechanical computer mounted on anti-aircraft guns which could automatically calculate where the target should be aimed at and used a mounted pointer to display this to the Predictor operators.
4 Combined Services Interrogation Reports. The National Archives, Kew. WO 208/3582.
5 Ibid.
6 Ibid.
7 Ibid.
8 Ibid.
9 Ibid.
10 Ibid.
11 Ibid.
12 Ibid.
13 Ibid.
14 Ibid.
15 Ibid.
16 Ibid.

three

SAFER SHORES

FROM CAPTURE TO CAMP

Processing new POWs was an arduous business. First they had to be transported to a holding area from where they had been captured – there were such places in Belgium and, later on, in British-occupied France. Here men could be treated for disease, searched, questioned and prepared for transport to England.

Journeying by boat, they arrived in London where they would be interviewed once more and assessed both on their political leanings and whether they may be able to provide useful information. The London Cage was the usual first stop for these men, where initial interviews determined where they would head next. Grading was not always done at this point – there were just too many men to process and it was expected that the camps themselves would assess the men more accurately once they arrived. Those men who were not to be held at the London Cage for further interrogation were dispersed by train to various locations.

In the early days of the war Britain had no interest in holding prisoners, so most were immediately shipped to Canada and America. This caused outrage among the Germans who feared the transport ships would be targeted by their own U-boats. Many men had been submarine crew before capture and they now realised with dismay that they could become the target of their own comrades. Indeed, British ships transporting Germans to America were attacked and sunk and fatalities were recorded.

Before long the British realised they were receiving too many prisoners to keep shipping them to America, so the decision was made to develop camps in England, Scotland, Wales and Ireland.

A detailed report concerning an Italian POW camp set up at Royston, Hertfordshire, gives a clear idea about how camps were expected to be arranged:

> The camp site is situated about 40 feet from the main Royston/Baldock road, about a quarter of a mile from the centre of the town. The site consists of a double-wired cage, one part for the prisoners approximately 350 x 150 feet, and one part for the guards approximately 200 x 150 feet. [1]

The site was expected to house 300 prisoners and 80 guards, but was only to be used during the summer when the prisoners might be employed in agricultural work nearby. The accommodation was to be Nissen huts with drainage trenches dug for the cooking and ablutions huts, while water was to be supplied by the Royston Waterworks who had already laid pipes to connect the camp to the main system.

Sewage arrangements proved more problematical. Buckets and a urine trough would be provided, but the emptying of them was cause for concern in case the contents spread disease. Initially a farmer was called on to collect the buckets and empty their contents on his field for fertiliser, but when it was realised that the ground was very chalky it was feared the sewage may seep down and pollute the water system.

The military had arranged that urine would empty into a soak-away, but again health concerns over the risks posed by urinary typhoid carriers meant that, in the end, both the trough and buckets would have to be emptied on a daily basis by a contractor, who would take everything immediately back to the sewage works.

Arrangements were made that should a prisoner become ill they would be sent to the nearest EMS (Emergency Medical Services) hospital. But should the prisoner have an infectious disease they would be sent to the military hospital at Colchester.

Many camps did have their own hospital facilities, often staffed by medical personnel picked out from among the prisoners.

A LACK OF BRITISH SYMPATHY

While many people managed to overlook their newest neighbours' enemy status, not everyone was sympathetic to them. Some saw no need to treat the men well or for Britain to even concern itself with their welfare.

In 1944 a London vicar wrote an appeal in his local parish paper asking for comforts to be given to German prisoners who were confined in hospitals in the area. The Reverend H.G. Green in Ipswich responded to the appeal by sending a tin of rat poison with an explanatory note: 'Having seen your tender-hearted request for comforts for the blasphemers of God and butchers of men, I herewith send a small comfort which I am sure they will enjoy. I am sorry the tin is not full, but a small dose will do the trick.'[2]

The 'donation' caused a great deal of consternation among the diocese; Green quickly found himself in hot water and attempted to explain his behaviour to his congregation, saying that the appeal had made him very upset:

> These Germans have perpetrated vile acts of murder, terror and plunder, and their villainies beggar description. I have no doubt that people who make such appeals think that they are acting in accordance with the Sermon on the Mount and the teachings of St Paul; but I defy anyone to find me a single sentence in the Bible where I can be called upon to serve the enemies of God and man.

He said he intended the rat poison as a joke and that he felt the prisoners were lucky to receive what they already did.

Green's 'joke' was going to have wider repercussions as it seems the press caught wind of it. After receiving the note the London vicar passed it on to the Bishop of St Edmundsbury and Ipswich. He tried to minimise the damage by giving a statement to the newspapers:

> Mr Green must not be taken seriously. He was trying to be funny. In any view, it was a poor joke, cheap and vulgar. He is entitled to his own views, though they are very different from mine. There is nothing I can do beyond telling him that, in my judgement, his action has been most reprehensible, and has brought discredit to the church.

Green, however, seemed unaffected by the trouble he had caused; he told one local newspaper that he had received 267 letters in one day and that only a few were against his actions. In his view the actions of the general public justified his 'joke' and confirmed that many were feeling the same way. He said: 'I have received letters of congratulations from officers and men in the Army, Navy and Air Force, from doctors and from clergymen of all denominations.'

How truthful this statement was will remain uncertain, but it goes to show that not everyone was able to feel sympathetic to their unusual guests.

COMMUNICATIONS

A vital aspect of camp life was the ability for prisoners to receive and send messages, particularly to and from their families. Much anxiety could be caused by a prisoner's fears over his family's safety and this was recognised by the camp authorities. Provisions for Italian POWs to send or receive telegrams were arranged, though publicity about the service was kept to a minimum.

Where telegrams were sent for the Italians there were various procedures that the prisoners had to follow. The messages were to only be written in Italian or English and had to be kept to a maximum of twelve words. Only one message could be sent by a prisoner per month and only the number of the camp and 'Gt Britain' were to be written on the telegram. No locations were to be given.

If the prisoner was either in the Italian air force or naval services then their first telegram had to be initially sent to either the Admiralty or Air Ministry, who would require up to two months to process it. The instructions did not specify why this delay was necessary, but it was only a problem for the very first telegram the man either sent or received.

All messages arrived at Liverpool to be censored and could be delayed for ninety-six hours. However, despite the delays, which to the men must have at times seemed unbearable, communication was at least possible and it provided a vital link with prisoners and their home and helped to keep depression at bay during the long months in captivity.

The British authorities wanted to send the messages to Italy via Berne, Switzerland, even though this did mean they were in communication with an enemy country. They hoped that by sending them through a neutral administration this would raise no objections and intended telegrams to be sent to the Italian Red Cross in Rome.

ESCAPES

Camp life in Britain was far from harsh and, combined with being stuck on an island with no obvious transport off, this reduced men's inclination to attempt an escape. But there were still those who were determined to try.

In some cases the escape was attempted before capture, such as when a German pilot baled out of his crippled bomber over Britain in January 1943 and stole a car. He was caught driving inland from Ashford, Kent, and arrested at Maidstone.

In another example from the same month two German airmen escaped from a train while in transit from London to a prison camp. Still wearing their Nazi uniform but speaking good English, they were captured in the Woking district the next day. Their British armed guards had failed to notice their disappearance until the train had reached its destination.

Trains must have been good for absconding from as two Germans escaped while being transported through the North Midlands. Home Guards joined the search for the men, who were eventually recaptured a couple of days later.

In the Home Counties three Germans escaped from their camp; the description in the papers read: 'They are all aged between 20 and 23 and consist of two naval ratings and a merchant seaman. They were in dyed battledress, the customary prison camp dress.'[3]

While in the Isle of Man:

> After being at liberty for 44 hours, a 25-year-old German civil air pilot detainee was recaptured on a lonely road in the Isle of Man late on Monday. He had escaped from a hospital attached to an internment camp and when caught wore the uniform of a Dutch naval officer. Earlier in the day the man called at a country cottage for a glass of milk and the police were informed.[4]

Some escape plans were so audacious as to be almost unbelievable. On 22 January 1945 a German who escaped from the camp at Crewe was arrested at a service aerodrome at Bitteswell, Leicestershire, by RAF personnel. The man was attempting to get into a Wellington aircraft. Information had been previously received stating that the escapee could fly almost any British plane solo. On being searched the man was found to be wearing three pairs of underpants, between which was a piece of silk containing a rough map of England indicating the main towns and the road to the east coast.

Attempts to recapture escaped prisoners were hampered by the red tape that had to be dealt with before effective searches could be initiated. First the camp commandant had to notify the police; the police then telephoned the Home Office, who then had to send a telegram to the coastal chief constable, who in turn had to inform the immigrations officers, customs authorities and the coast guard. The result was that the Home Office had to issue 120 telegrams to all the various police forces across the country per escape. Despite the administrative nightmare this system caused it was not until 1946 that it was even contemplated that the situation should be changed, and that the Home Office should only inform Scotland Yard, who would then be responsible for telephoning the various police forces to inform them.

Careful reports of escapes and recaptures were maintained on a week-by-week basis. The reports provide interesting reading and evidence that escapes were regular but in relatively low numbers.

The report from the week ending 12 February 1945 stated that five Italians, twenty-five Germans and ten Russians had escaped. However, the number of prisoners that remained at large was far lower; only four Italians, two Germans and eight Russians had evaded capture.

The following week's report showed that a further four Italians, eight Germans and seventeen Russians had escaped, but the number that remained at large was very similar to the previous week: six Italians, two Germans and ten Russians.

A report from the week ending 12 March gives a better idea of the motives for the prisoners' escape attempts and also shows how the figures could be skewed. One Italian co-operator[5] was listed as escaped as he was absent from his camp for twenty-four hours before returning. Thirteen non-co-operator Italians had escaped, while two Germans went missing from a party of prisoners being sent back from a labour camp to a base camp. The prisoners had been deemed unsuitable for employment but did not want to return to the base camp and its tighter security so attempted an escape.

In fact, most escapes seem to have occurred, among the Germans at least, at the base camps. There had been eighty-six escapes from base camps, including seventy from the Bridgend officers' camp alone. At this camp two tunnels had been discovered in December 1944, but the prisoners were also working on a third and hoped that the two extra tunnels would act as a blind for the real one and could account for the soil scattered about the camp.

At the time of the report thirty-six men were still missing from the Bridgend camp, while a further forty-seven Germans and eight Italians were at large. Up until 20 March 1945, of 420 prisoners who had escaped only four remained at large.[6]

On 13 March the commandant of the POW camp at Crewe Hall, Crewe, discovered a similar tunnel measuring 30 yards long leading from a hut to the perimeter fence designed for a mass escape. Later a second tunnel was discovered in another hut. Both were found before being completed and the attempts were thwarted.

The police were notified when escapes occurred but were hampered by restrictions on the use of the police wireless. An ongoing debate raged as to whether the police should be allowed to use their wireless systems after an escape. While some thought this would speed progress, others connected with the Security Service had evidence that information could be leaked by intercepted wireless calls.

Hampered or not, eventually all escapees from the Bridgend camp were rounded up. Shortly after, the ban was lifted on the use of the police wireless and now escape reports could be broadcast across the whole country.

During 1945 it was agreed that not only would the number of escapes and nationality of the German prisoners be reported, but also their political gradings. So on the week ending 10 December, it was recorded that five Germans, unscreened (meaning they had not been classified yet) and one German ranked as Grade B had escaped. However, six unscreened Germans and one Grade B German had been recaptured that week.

Unscreened Germans caused a lot of apprehension among the British authorities. Some wanted to classify any such escaped prisoner as Grade C+ (ardent Nazi), while others indicated this was an unfair assumption. The general rule was that no prisoner of Grade C+ should be employed in working parties that were involved in war work. However, by the number of unscreened prisoners that were escaping from labour camps or parties it would seem likely that some must have slipped through. This raised a wholly new and unexpected question: if these men were unscreened, how could the camp commandants be sure they were not employing ardent Nazis in sensitive work?

In fact, by 1945, restrictions on the use of 'black' POWs were being loosened. The Air Ministry had plans to use a number of C+ prisoners in some of their secret establishments and asked for information on the number of 'black' prisoners who remained at large to ensure they could avoid contacts being made with the prisoners in their employ.

THE INGENIOUS AND THE DELUDED

Some escape attempts could be remarkable in their audacity and in the confidence of the escapees. The ploys they used were often complex, carefully constructed and sometimes even accompanied by forged documents.

In November 1944 a German was found and captured on a Huntingdonshire airfield. He had intended to steal a Mosquito and fly back to Germany. Though not listed as a 'special class' prisoner, as he was not actually a pilot, he believed he could fly the plane from his time served on the ground staff in the German air force.

If that prisoner had undue confidence in himself, a group of three Germans who escaped from a Monmouthshire camp were even more brazen in their attempt. They were arrested at Holyhead on 23 November, claiming to be French seamen from Brittany who were heading for the French consul in Dublin for instructions. They had documents containing photographs that they claimed to be 'cartes di dendite'. One spoke French in a rapid way but had a limited vocabulary and, when questioned by a native of Brest on local topography, struggled to answer correctly.

The documents were obvious forgeries and the men eventually confessed to making them in the camp. The French on the documents was poor; a stamp on them that said *Etat Francais* had been made by rubbing over a French franc.

After their escape the men had changed a 1,000-franc note at Chepstow and sold a watch for £12. They had stayed overnight at Birmingham and Liverpool before reaching Holyhead. At Liverpool they had bought second-hand clothing and had their photographs taken for the forged documents. The men apparently intended to travel to Dublin so that they might be interned in a camp in Eire.

Some prisoners were perpetually trying to escape. One such case was a German airman named von Werra. He was captured early on in the war and initially interned in Britain. There he made two unsuccessful escape attempts until, in 1941, he was shipped with a contingency of other prisoners to Canada. There he escaped again and made his way into the USA, which at the time was considered by the British to be a 'neutral' country (though technically this was inaccurate as America was already providing Britain with materials and loans for the fight against Germany).

The British authorities were instantly concerned; von Werra knew things they did not want him to reveal and could pose a serious security risk if he made it back to Germany, but legally the treatment by a neutral country of another nation's prisoners was a grey area. When British prisoners had escaped Germany and made it to Holland they were interned. However, in other countries they were simply released on parole. Despite the British pressing for von Werra to be imprisoned, the Americans released him on bail in New York.

Politically and legally there was very little the British could do other than to try and arrange a treaty between themselves and the US regarding POW treatment. One British general spoke bluntly and said that there was no chance of the von Werra problem being resolved unless a gunman was hired to shoot him down – to which he hastily added that he would not like to see this happen as von Werra was a 'stout man and a good soldier'.

Of course, von Werra eventually made his way to Germany, thus fulfilling all the British concerns. Von Werra's escape seems to have been the most politically charged among those prisoners who eluded their Canadian guards. There were other attempts, including those of several Germans who tried to swim away from the HMT *Queen Mary* that was transporting them to Canada, but these men were captured. In the end, it would only be a matter of months before the USA joined the war after the Japanese attack on Pearl Harbor on 7 December 1941. No longer a neutral country, and with their own POW camps, they were to be less lenient on escapees from Canada and the British could feel some of their worries lift.

The Bridgend Escape

On the night of 10 March 1945, fifty-six Germans escaped from the Island Farm, Bridgend POW camp. They had excavated a tunnel under the barbed-wire fence. At 5.20 a.m. on 11 March two of the escapees were apprehended by local police 4 miles from the camp at Llanharan. They were returned directly to their camp commandant and interviewed.

The men revealed that the prisoners had escaped in groups of ten to twelve, splitting into pairs as soon as they were outside the fence and heading in different directions. By 17 March all but eight prisoners had been recaptured. These final few had managed to evade military and police cordons at Glamorgan and were eventually found at various locations. Two were captured at the Severn Tunnel Junction, two at Eastleigh, Southampton, and the final four at Castle Bromich, Warwickshire. These last four had stolen a car at Bridgend and driven it as far as Blakeney before abandoning it.

The audacious escape plan, and the success of those prisoners that had eluded the cordons, intrigued the authorities and careful questioning revealed the weaknesses in the British camp system. The prisoners who had escaped the cordon had made for high ground at the outset to get an understanding of the lay of the land. They had managed to hoard enough food from their rations to last them up to a fortnight while at liberty. Prior to the escape a GHQ inspection had noted that the men were stockpiling food from their daily ration, but this seemed unavoidable as the Geneva Convention laid down that prisoners were to have the same rations as base troops. The rations were clearly large enough to enable the prisoners to keep some back.

The prisoners had made considerable use of whatever transport they could find. Aside from the four who had stolen a car, others took bicycles and some travelled around using the railways, boarding mineral trains to avoid being seen and carrying improvised maps and compasses.

On 15 March questions were being asked in the House of Commons about the escape. The Secretary of State for War, Mr A. Henderson, was grilled on the matter. In a statement, he gave different numbers of escapees to those recorded in the official reports, saying sixty-seven German POWs had escaped, sixty-five of them being officers. He added that forty-eight had been recaptured. The escape had happened at 4 a.m., when prisoners had made their way down a 20-yard-long tunnel, the entrance of which, the minister explained, had been hidden in the corner of a living hut. An 18in square of 4in-thick concrete had been cut out and camouflaged to disguise the tunnel. Henderson stated that a Court of Inquiry was due to examine the case and he refused to answer any further questions on the subject of the implements the prisoners used, or how the excess soil was concealed, until the inquiry had been finished. Other ministers wanted to know if the site of the camp was going to be questioned, but Henderson was evasive on the matter.

It was not the first time Mr Henderson had found himself under scrutiny in the House of Commons. The previous December (1944) questions had been asked about the escape of over ninety Italian prisoners from a camp in west Scotland. Mr Henderson assured the House that of the ninety-seven men who had escaped, eighty-nine had been recaptured.

Unsatisfied, Sir T. Moore put it to him: 'As these escapes are becoming disconcertingly frequent, is the minister satisfied that security measures in prisoner-of-war camps are satisfactory?'

Henderson was annoyed with the implied suggestion that the situation was becoming worse and confirmed that he felt security measures were sufficient.

It was not just in the House of Commons that questions were being asked about escapes. The press had also taken an interest in reporting POW breakouts and the *Daily Express* ran a piece in December 1944, at the same time as Henderson was being interrogated on Italian escapes, about a mass escape planned by German prisoners.

How the newspaper had obtained its information was unclear and the Security Service was not interested in pursuing the matter. The *Daily Express* ran two further pieces in December discussing the 'special measures' being taken at Fascist-Italian and German POW camps, as German captives were arriving in Britain with 'carefully prepared plans for coordinated escapes'.

The claim in the *Daily Express* was that prior to leaving Germany men were given detailed escape plans that differed depending on whether they were a soldier, sailor or airman. Certain men were chosen to be escape leaders and were given the task, if captured, of organising Nazi cells within camps and leading the break-out.

German pilots were said to be given instructions to capture British aircraft or sabotage airfields after their escape and sailors were said to be told to get to the nearest port and 'seize or sabotage ships'. The paper claimed that German pilots were taught to fly British planes by practising on captured Allied aircraft and sailors were taught to navigate British ships.

Soldiers, the *Daily Express* continued, would never attempt a break-out alone, but would always take either sailors or pilots with them as otherwise they would have no means of getting away from England. Their main goal was to leave England with as much information as possible for Hitler.

The article went on stating that those men who tried to escape were 'always found to have an extraordinary knowledge of the country. Even those who profess to speak no English are able to ask the way and make simple replies to questions – enough to pass themselves off as Poles or Czechs.' Their extensive knowledge was said to come from memorising maps of the areas where the prison camps were situated and the routes to the nearest airfield.

'Some German prisoners have been able to draw amazingly accurate maps of the district where they are imprisoned from memory ... They have been specially trained to notice the country, the trees, the soil, any buildings which they can see for "local" architecture, even the names of public houses.'

Furthermore, it was said several would-be escapees had figured out which district they were in by the brewers' names on public houses when being taken through local towns in lorries. Then they chose a pilot or sailor to lead the escape depending on whether they were nearer an airfield or a port.

To emphasise its point, on 18 December the newspaper ran a piece on an attempted mass escape by a U-boat crew and Luftwaffe pilots, all fanatical Nazis being held in south-west England. The Germans were said to have been prepared to lose half their number in attempting to get away. The *Daily Express* reported that the prisoners had ruthlessly planned to butcher the guards, seize the armoury and form up at an assembly point outside the camp before attacking a nearby airfield with hopes of capturing a plane. The plot was foiled by a British guard who, while watching the camp from a raised tower, noticed prisoners 'furtively' conversing among themselves. Five or six Germans would gather together and talk, while another appeared to be standing as a lookout. Then the group would disperse and each prisoner would talk to another group of five Germans. Suspicions aroused, all the camp guards were ordered to watch the men more closely and any who understood German were to mix with the prisoners.

Shortly before dawn one morning, a prisoner was seen leaving his Nissen hut and heading for an outbuilding. There he met with another prisoner and exchanged a piece of paper. When it was confiscated it was discovered to contain last-minute instructions for an escape plan. The plot discovered, camp life returned to normal. The *Daily Express* reported:

> This afternoon the prisoners were standing behind the barbed wire discussing the English people out for an afternoon walk along the country road. Only a small hawthorn hedge and the barbed wire separated them from the public. Their washing was hanging on improvised lines and the prisoners who were not watching this afternoon's football match hung about aimlessly.

The *Daily Express* carried another article on 21 December about an attempted mutiny at a POW camp. It revealed that on the previous Monday (19 December) thirteen German officers escaped from a camp at Penkridge, Staffordshire; the remaining officers had stayed up all Tuesday night stamping on floors, beating tattoos on walls and 'booing, hissing and taunting the guards', shouting at them: 'You'll never catch them!'

The following morning, German officers detailed to shovel coal drew into a formation and approached the gate guards, waving their shovels and shouting. The British sergeant-major ordered the guard to level their Sten guns and be ready to fire. Upon hearing this, the officers disbanded and went back to their work. Further guards with fixed bayonets and Sten guns were detailed about the camp but no more trouble ensued.

The paper was careful to make it clear that non-commissioned German officers housed in adjoining compounds took no part in the mutiny and were as friendly as usual with the guards, bartering wooden toys they had made for cigarettes.

The men who had actually escaped had done so in thick fog and consisted of Luftwaffe pilots, merchant navy officers and infantry officers from the Western Front. They had cut through the barbed-wire fence with weapons they had secretly fashioned in their huts. With some dressed in civilian clothes, some in field grey and some in the dark blue uniform of the Luftwaffe, they made their way to the nearest main road.

It was an hour later that the escape was discovered and camp guards followed the trail with the camp's German shepherd dog across country until they reached a river – on the opposite side of which the dog lost the trail. The Germans had scattered, two being recaptured at Walsall, two at Wolverhampton, six at Derby and two at Liverpool. One merchant navy officer remained free but, although dressed in civilian clothes, spoke little English.

Four of the men caught at Derby were travelling in a stolen car which ran out of petrol. Police Constable Richards spotted the stranded men in their German uniforms and approached them. Asking if they needed help, he was told they were Poles on leave trying to get to Nottingham.

Richards offered to give them a ride to a place where they could get a lift. The men accepted the offer and got into the PC's car, whereupon he drove them to the police station. As they were walking into the building three broke away but were soon recaptured.

The *News Chronicle* gave more information about the two Germans caught at Liverpool, who were apparently trying to board a ferry bound for Eire. When Police Constable John Roberts spotted them watching boats cross the Mersey he was 'struck by the unusual trouser legs under their civilian overcoats'. Speaking to them, they responded in broken English; Roberts then pulled aside the collar of one of the men and saw the German uniform and Wehrmacht badge.

After their recapture some of the escapees were found to be carrying razor-sharp knives, civilian clothes and supplies of bully beef and bread.

Escape or Die

Unfortunately not all escapes had such peaceful conclusions. There were incidents where men were shot trying to escape and the cases investigated by the military courts. Several examples from 1945 show how tensions could rise and lead to deaths within the camp.

On 9 February 1945 Robert Speilmann, a member of the German medical service at Glen Mill POW camp, was told by the camp commandant that his friend and colleague Paul Hartmann had been shot and killed. Hartmann had arrived in the camp in 1944 and as the two men were both in the medical service they became friends. It was Speilmann's unpleasant duty to have to visit the mortuary and identify his friend's body. Hartmann had been killed by a bullet to the right eye; the coroner suggested it had come from a rifle.

Before Hartmann's death on 7 February the commandant of the camp, Captain W.L. James, had decided to hold a count of the prisoners following a number of escapes. He knew several prisoners had escaped but not exactly how many, so at 8.30 a.m. he began with a routine roll call that continued until midday. The prisoners, however, were intent on preventing an accurate count in order to mask the number of men who had escaped. They were obstructive and awkward and Captain James was unsatisfied with the final count.

At 2 p.m. Captain James ordered a more careful count. The men were brought out in groups, beginning with Allied nationals and then working through the German army ranks, ending with the SS. The men once again tried to make life difficult and avoided coming outside by moving very slowly. It was 4.30 p.m. by the time everyone who could come outside had done so. The men remaining inside were the sick personnel, numbering about 250.

The camp at Glen Mill included a portion of a road called Constantine Street. Half the assembled prisoners were put in an enclosed portion of the street; the other half, deemed by Captain James to be low risk, were put in an open portion of the road.

As the afternoon progressed it began to rain and the Germans resented being outside in the bad weather. They began catcalling to the posted sentries and shouting abuse. Captain James stood in Constantine Street to keep an eye on them. He left his place at 5 p.m. to get his officers to hurry up as he wanted the men back inside. He was gone no more than five minutes, yet on his return found a prisoner lying dead in the street, shot by the sentry at post No 5.

All afternoon Captain James had experienced problems with the prisoners trying to interfere with the sentries' patrols. There were around 1,500 men outside and those at the back were pushing on the ones in front, forcing them forward until they would overrun the sentries. If this was to happen, the sentry would have no option but to open fire and a mass escape would have been inevitable.

Despite persistent attempts by the prisoners to cause trouble, Captain James had kept the men in line with threats; he told the court he was not allowed to use force, so verbal threats were all he had. It seems that when he left, even if it was only briefly, some of the prisoners had seized their chance and pushed the group forward.

The sentry of post No 5 had opened fire, leaving one man lying dead and four more injured. The dead man was identified as Paul Hartmann, one of the protected personnel who should have been standing 200 yards away at the rear of the group. How he came to be at the front Captain James didn't know.

Nor had he heard a shot fired, though with the amount of noise the prisoners were making it would have been difficult to hear. The sentry at post No 5 had an awkward route as he crossed over between the two groups of prisoners Captain James had organised. Hartmann had been among the unconfined prisoners who James felt would not cause any trouble. He had died in that section and his body lay on the path that was part of the sentry's patrol.

Hartmann had been shot in the head from a range of 50 yards. The bullet had struck bone, breaking off fragments which had formed secondary missiles and caused a large part of the damage. If the range had been further the velocity of the bullet would have decreased and the impact would have been less forceful.

The sentry who had shot Hartmann was named J.A. Jaffray, a gunner in the Royal Artillery. He had gone on duty at 1 p.m. During the afternoon the prisoners had been restless and Jaffray had repeatedly told them to stand back from the sentry post. All the time the POWs were booing and sneering at the sentries. At 4 p.m. the prisoners headed towards Jaffray again. At first he did nothing as they were not on his beat, but they carried on approaching so he gave the signal for them to move back. They ignored him.

Still jeering and booing at the sentry the prisoners carried on. Jaffray called 'Halt!' three times and was ignored, so he loaded his gun. The prisoners started laughing. Jaffray cried 'Halt!' a second time; again the Germans laughed at him. So he fired.

He shot from the hip and attempted to aim over the men's heads to scare them rather than to hurt anyone. He was in danger of being overrun but had no desire to kill anyone so aimed deliberately up. In this he was disobeying military orders which stated a sentry should shoot to kill.

As he fired a man stepped forward and the bullet went straight through him. He fell to the ground. Jaffray contended that if the men had stopped when he ordered them to the bullet would have gone over their heads and no one would have been hurt. After the shot the prisoners retreated. Jaffray was certain he only fired one shot. Besides Hartmann, several men were injured.

Another sentry and a member of the camp staff confirmed that the prisoners were advancing on Jaffray and they had heard him shout out for them to stop before a single shot was fired. The sentry, however, said that the words he heard Jaffray use were not 'Halt!' but 'Get back or I shall fire!' The camp interpreter agreed that the prisoners had been abusive and unco-operative. The prisoners moved slowly to hamper the count, despite the camp interpreter telling them that if they speeded up they could get back indoors quicker. He heard one man refer to the camp staff in German as 'these swine'.

A German named Fritz Scheer gave his side of events. He was in the seventh of eight groups to be put into Constantine Street. He said the men had not been told to stay in their groups and, due to the large numbers of men coming into the area, he was forced down to within 20m of the top gate of the compound. As more and more prisoners entered, Scheer found himself pushed down the road until he was four or five rows from the front. Twice a sentry told the men to step back and they did, but then a surge from the back of the group forced the men forward again. Scheer was jumping from foot to foot trying to keep warm when he heard a shot fired. Something hit his face. When Scheer touched it with his hand he realised it was blood and bone. Splinters of bone had cut his cheek and shards of metal had struck his eye and nose. One piece, the size of the tip of a pencil, was stuck in his skin. The metal had come from the bullet which had shattered upon hitting Hartmann. Afterwards Scheer, considering his wounds were not serious, went for a meal. He told the inquiry the crowd were singing old folk songs and love songs, nothing provocative or offensive.

Another prisoner, Fritz Hoenisch, told a similar story. He added, however, that the crowd had been making a lot of noise 'singing and shouting at birds that were flying above us', but that at the time of the shooting the crowd was silent.

One German, Hans Huebner, saw Jaffray lower his gun and fumble with the bolt. Through an interpreter, he said: 'I had a premonition he was going to shoot and was going to tell my comrades, but thought it was impossible for him to fire on unarmed men – most of whom had their hands in their pockets. Hardly had the thought crossed my mind then there was a shot.'

The evidence of the men and the post-mortem showed that the bullet which killed Hartmann had disintegrated upon impact with bone, peppering the men near him with fragments of metal. This became a contentious point during the inquiry. One British expert said that he had seen similar destruction of bullets when fired from a short range and it had nothing to do with the quality of the bullet.

A German expert, however, contested this saying he felt the bullet was in some way defective to have shattered and caused so much damage inside Hartmann's head. He put it down to the bullets being loaded and unloaded from the gun repeatedly and not changed often enough. He said: 'In Germany the sentry's ammunition is changed frequently.'

Whether or not the quality of the bullet had an impact on Hartmann's death remained unanswered, though the other men would not have been struck with shards of metal had it remained intact.

The verdict of the inquiry was that Jaffray had acted with justification. It was also felt that his actions had prevented the prisoners from rioting or escaping – an action that would have caused the other sentries to open fire and many men to be injured or killed. Opinion was that Jaffray had not intended to kill Hartmann and had he not stepped forward the shot would have gone over his head. They were unconvinced with the German evidence that the bullet was defective.

The inquiry concluded by saying Hartmann's death was the result of compound fracture of the skull caused by a rifle bullet and instigated by the prisoners ignoring warnings to move back and Jaffray's concern that he was about to be overrun.

Not everyone was satisfied by this verdict; the camp leader at camp 176, Fedor Tippner, felt Hartmann's death unnecessary and wanted to protest. In a neatly written letter sent directly to the War Office, where it was translated, he spelt out his complaint.

He stated that the second prisoner count was simply an excuse to make the men stand outside in the rain and cold all day. The camp leader saw this as a punitive punishment for the fact some men had escaped and argued that this was against the Geneva Convention. He also believed that the number of armed guards surrounding the men was far in excess of what was needed for a simple roll call.

To pass the hours of waiting, the camp leader went on, the men sang songs and told jokes. At one point an officer pushed them back by waving a pistol at them and striking men in the chest with it. He then walked over to a sentry and spoke with him before leaving. Presumably this sentry was Jaffray. The camp leader said that Jaffray had then begun to load his gun and aim it at the men's heads. With no provocation, the letter emphatically persisted, he shot at the men. One fell down dead, another wounded. Five other men received injuries from shards of the bullet, proving that the ammunition was defective.

He declared that after the incident all the other sentries turned their guns on the men and an officer manning a machine gun on a hill levelled it at them. When Germans tried to help their fallen comrades they were forcefully ordered back.

Even more damning, the camp leader alleged that men, even those who were wounded, were beaten and abused as they fell in for the roll call. He felt that the gun shot that killed Hartmann had been deliberate since there was no provocation and that certain people on the camp staff should be removed 'so that the German inmates of this camp, may again have the feeling of being correctly treated, thus establishing co-operation with the English camp authorities which when working without friction serves best the interest of both parties concerned'.

It was a very different perspective on the events of 7 February. However, there were no other complaints of ill-treatment from the prisoners and some of what Tippner wrote contradicted what other German witnesses had said. They had previously said the crowd was making a lot of noise and repeatedly moved towards Jaffray's position.

The court dismissed the complaint. They concluded that Jaffray was not to blame for Hartmann's death as he was following his orders, which he actually disobeyed by attempting to fire over the heads of the prisoners. They did feel, though, that Captain James had brandished a revolver at the crowd of prisoners in an attempt to scare them into stepping back. While they did not consider this a disciplinary matter, they did feel it 'lacked dignity'.

As in most of the cases presented to the courts, the prisoners usually denied they had done anything to justify the shooting; they attempted to present themselves as model prisoners and while not all of their allegations can be dismissed, clearly they were going to stick together and defend their actions. The truth in the majority of these cases probably lies somewhere between the two sides of the story.

ANOTHER DEVIZES ESCAPE

Often men attempted escapes either alone or in pairs, but occasionally large parties tried a mass escape. Such was the case on 27 February 1945 at the POW camp at Devizes, Wiltshire.

The camp was manned by the Polish guard, Coy. At 4 p.m. the camp interpreter was told by a prisoner informant that an escape was being planned for that night. The camp adjutant was warned and he arranged for extra sentries to be posted.

At 11.45 p.m. the Polish sentries reported that they could hear someone tampering with the wire but could not locate their position. A search party was organised, the sentries were informed what was happening and the group, consisting of the orderly officer, provost staff, the camp interpreter and a Polish NCO, began walking around the perimeter fence.

After only fifteen minutes two prisoners were found in the ditch of 'C' compound, having climbed through the wire that confined them to their own area. The Polish sentries were told to cover them and the prisoners ordered to lie down while the party continued into 'C' compound to locate any further escapees.

Before they could get very far a Polish sentry started to fire. There were more prisoners loose in the compound and the sentry had opened fire when one disobeyed his orders. This prisoner was killed outright. Several others had been concealed but when the firing started they began to run and three were wounded. In total, the search party found seven POWs, plus the dead man.

The escapees turned out to be all members of the Luftwaffe. About half had been in the camp for several months, while the remainder were recent arrivals from another camp. Together they had formed an 'air army', two of them being pilots, and they intended to escape the camp and make their way to the nearest airfield to steal a plane.

The men were woefully under-prepared for the endeavour. They had no food supplies and only had a vague idea of how far it was to the airfield. But they had managed to obtain a large pair of wire cutters.

After the disturbance the entire camp was paraded and a man count done. One further German had been injured when a stray bullet entered his hut and struck him.

Another mass escape was attempted on 16 February at camp 17 in Sheffield. It was around 11 p.m. when Private Butler approached a relief sentry and told him he could hear noises near the north main wall outside the perimeter fence. Neither man had a torch and the night was dark and cloudy.

They made their way down the fence until they reached a fixed search-light. The relief sentry turned the searchlight around to face the wall. Immediately he saw a POW against the wall. He challenged him and the man put up his hands and walked towards them. The sentries made it clear that he should stay by the searchlight while it was swung along the wall.

The sentries spotted more prisoners in the beam of the light. They challenged them and the men began to run in the direction of the main gate. Another warning was issued, but they continued to run and the sentries fired, though failed to hit anyone.

They then swung the light back and saw two more prisoners getting off the ground. Aware they had been spotted, the men started to run towards the football field. The sentries fired and at least one man was hit as he fell and lay on the ground groaning loudly. His companion put up his hands and walked towards the sentries. He was made to understand that he was to bring his companion near to the wire.

Once there, the uninjured POW began shouting out and several other prisoners appeared and approached the sentries. In total they had captured eight men, including the badly injured man.

The injured man was Alfred Steinbacher; at a Court of Inquiry hearing into the matter he gave evidence about that night. Steinbacher had decided to escape with several companions and at around 8 p.m. or 9 p.m. that night the perimeter wire near a road was cut. The work was repeatedly interrupted by the patrols of the sentries.

Eventually, however, a suitable hole was created and the men crept through in single file. Steinbacher was either the fifth or sixth man through. Several people had joined the party since the plan was conceived, but it was the seven original plotters who made it through the fence before the alarm was raised.

The prisoners attempted to spread out and hide along a wall and behind the sentry post. The night was still and it was hard for the prisoners to keep quiet enough so as not to be noticed. The searchlight was swung about and Steinbacher assumed someone had been spotted when shots were fired. It was after those prisoners who had escaped attempted to get back in the camp that Steinbacher was shot.

The court felt the sentries had been justified in their actions and that Steinbacher had received his injuries while trying to escape. He had been shot in the chest and abdomen and the injuries were officially recorded as serious.

There was one other man who had been shot. His name was Hans Kunz and he had received a bullet wound to his upper arm. Fortunately the injury was not serious and the bullet was simply removed.

Another German death happened during the night of 13 March 1945. The deceased was named Fink and he was spotted by a sentry standing in the wire surrounding the compound. The wire had been cut and Fink was clambering through it. The sentry challenged Fink, who merely mumbled something in German that the sentry did not understand. He challenged him again, telling him to come back through the wire. When Fink failed to obey the sentry opened fire and Fink was severely wounded and died a few minutes after being admitted to hospital.

A post-mortem showed he had been struck by several bullets. One bullet had gone through his left elbow, another had hit the tip of his right shoulder and exited out his chest, and the third had struck his left shoulder and also exited out the chest. He had also taken a shot in the chest. The cause of death was due to multiple gunshot wounds and loss of blood.

Unlike some of the other cases there were no other prisoners involved in the escape and, after several witnesses were questioned, the Court of Inquiry found that the sentry had acted according to his orders. No wire cutters were ever found on Fink or near him, though two holes were found cut in the wire. Whether he had assistance or was just taking a chance remained a mystery.

A similar incident resulted in the death of Herbert Lisser, a prisoner at Monrush camp in Northern Ireland. The Court of Inquiry assembled on 3 April 1945 at the camp where Lisser was shot.

On 19 March a German prisoner had attempted to climb through the boundary wire of the camp just before 10 p.m. He was shot by Private Short, who was stationed as a 'prowler' between sentry posts 6 and 10. The German's body was lying on the ground midway between posts 6 and 7. Short was shining his torch on him and was armed with the Sten gun he had been issued with upon going on sentry duty.

Short gave evidence as to what had happened. He had been patrolling for about half an hour when he noticed two POWs standing opposite post No 7, apparently trying to attract the attention of the sentry. Short spoke with the sentry who had already noticed the men, then he moved on to post No 6. A few minutes later, as he returned, he saw a group of POWs around the prisoners' latrine. He then spotted two more POWs who appeared to be patrolling between sentry posts 6 and 7. His suspicions aroused by this peculiar behaviour, Short went to investigate. The night was dark and it was raining. Short walked as far as post 7 then doubled back instead of carrying on to post 10. It was as he returned to post 6 that he caught sight of a man trying to crawl through the outside boundary wire.

Short called out, 'Halt or I fire!' and blew his whistle to raise the alarm. He repeated the warning but the German did not stop, and so, in Short's own words, he 'fired to kill'. He shot a burst of eight rounds and heard the person cry out. The POW was seriously wounded but Short continued to cover him with the gun until the duty officer arrived. The POW had cut the wire using a pair of homemade wire cutters that were still lying beside him. Lissor later died from his wounds.

The court was of the opinion that Short had been justified in shooting Lissor. They did make it clear, however, that three warnings should have been given, but understood that under the conditions, with the POW almost free of the wire, Short did not have time to call another warning. Short was deemed to have acted appropriately and Lissor, by attempting to escape, was considered entirely to blame for the fatal injuries he sustained.

Another case from Scotland did not result in fatalities, but two POWs were wounded at camp 188. This incident happened on the night of 18 or 19 April 1945.

A section of prisoner huts in camp 188 were under a special curfew operating from 9 p.m. on 18 April to 6.30 a.m. the following morning. The prisoners were not to wander more than 5 yards from their huts during this time and if they did the sentries were ordered to shoot at them. Latrine buckets were placed at the end of the huts so the men had no reason to wander further afield.

At 9.25 p.m. two sentries shot at two prisoners; both men were injured and removed for treatment. One of the sentries reported that he had seen a prisoner walking away from his hut and shouted at the man to get back inside. He was ignored and the man proceeded towards a line of trees 50 yards from the hut. The sentry then opened fire on him. The second sentry told a similar story, that he had seen a prisoner leave his hut and head for the trees; when warned he still did not return to the hut and was fired upon. The sentries were considered to have been following orders and no blame was to be attached to them.

In another inquiry the sentry was considered slightly less blameless. On 22 April 1945, Hans Schulze and Karl Schwarz were shot at and injured by Polish sentry Pietrowski at the POW camp at Comrie, Perthshire. Pietrowski had seen several Germans standing outside their huts and he had ordered them back inside. They all obeyed but a few minutes later four men came outside again. Pietrowski told them to go back inside three times, but they took no notice of the order – instead they laughed at him.

The sentry gave the command again and told them if they did not obey he would fire. They still laughed at him. Pietrowski kept them covered with his gun for five minutes, then one of the men bent down and appeared to be picking up a stone. Presuming the man might be intending to throw it at him, he opened fire and shot three times into the group.

One German fell while the others ran away. One man was shot in the cheek, the bullet arching at a left angle through his mouth and knocking out two teeth. Another man was shot in the neck. The sentry reported what had happened to a Polish officer at 10.20 p.m. and the injured men, one being the camp interpreter, were taken to hospital. They each denied that they had laughed at the sentry or heard any warnings.

The prisoners were all supposed to be locked in their huts by 10 p.m. The huts were locked by a British policeman assigned to the camp. On the night in question, however, the huts in 'D' compound where the men had been shot were yet to be locked.

Pietrowski told the court that they had definitely been laughing at him, but it was only when one bent down that he opened fire. He was asked if he spoke German and confessed that he only knew a little. He was then asked if the Germans had actually spoken to him and he answered they had not.

'How do you know they were laughing at you?' The cross-examiner asked bluntly.

Pietrowski answered that they were looking at him when they laughed and that he had only followed orders. Two other Polish sentries confirmed they had heard warnings issued and the Germans laughing.

However, a German POW witness said he had been leaving the lavatories near one of the huts when he heard shots fired. He told the court he had definitely heard no warnings. Another German who was inside hut No 9 during the incident and watching out of a window told a similar story, that he had seen the sentry aim and fire but had heard no warnings. Another German who was among the group that were shot at stated that they had been playing between huts 24 and 25. Schwarz, the injured prisoner, was dancing when shots were suddenly fired. Schwarz was hit and took cover behind hut 24. Again it was said no warning was heard and, as the huts had yet to be locked up, the Germans felt they were doing nothing wrong by being outside.

Another of the Germans in the dancing party told the same story, saying he was standing next to Schulze, the other injured man. He reckoned he had told the men it was time to go inside and had hardly spoken when shots rang out. He dropped to the ground and saw Schulze hit. He also told the court that no one had bent down to pick anything up.

Further questioning asked whether it was Pietrowski's duty to make sure the men were in the huts. He answered that his orders stated that he must ensure no one was outside after 10 p.m. When asked who locked the huts, he answered simply 'the British'. He then told the court that he had not seen the British lock up the huts in 'D' compound before the incident.

The court then went back to the point when he had fired. He told them he had been aiming at all the men until one had bent down, then he had aimed solely at him. When asked if any stone was thrown, he said none was and that he had opened fire as soon as the prisoner bent down.

The authorities were in two minds about the situation. On the one hand, they felt that Pietrowski had been following his orders as laid down, but on the other they considered the matter could have been handled better without resorting to firing on the men. The evidence that the men had been laughing at the sentry and that warnings were given was contradictory and, as they had been only standing just outside their huts and the evening was still light, opening fire was viewed as an error of judgement.

The District Council defended the sentry. The camp at Comrie, Perthshire, was rather notorious for the many ardent Nazis and difficult prisoners that were housed there. Under the circumstances it seemed to them the sentry had acted appropriately. In the end the matter was laid to rest, the prisoners seen largely at fault for not obeying camp rules, but with reservations about Pietrowski's judgement.

On its own, the court's decision might seem lenient. But there was another reason for them to be suspicious of the German POWs' motives for being outside and for Pietrowski to believe they were going to throw a stone at him. Only the night before, on 21 April 1945, another German named Heinrich Schwarz had been shot and killed by a Polish guard.

The guard was named Sergeant Benke and on 21 April he was on his inspection rounds. At 11 a.m. a stone was thrown at him and the same happened at 4 p.m. He took no notice and made no report. At 7.35 p.m., while Benke was taking a report from a sentry, three POWs appeared, walking close to the wire fence. One picked up a stone and threw it at Benke. It hit him and the Germans began to run away. Benke ordered them to stop three times, following them as they ran along the fence. When they did not stop he drew his revolver and fired four rounds.

Schwarz, the prisoner who had thrown the stone, fell down. He had been shot through the head and later died on his way to the hospital in Edinburgh. The sentry could back up Benke's story that the prisoner had thrown a stone at him. But the Germans denied this, even going as far as to say Schwarz had his hands in his pockets at the time. More damningly, they said that Benke had shot at Schwarz when he was already lying on the ground.

The court did not look favourably on Benke, who had previously been involved in another shooting incident. They felt it was unfortunate the previous stone-throwing incidents had not been reported, but were satisfied that a deliberate attempt was being made to bait the sergeant. Benke was known to be strict and had also witnessed his wife and children being murdered before him by the Gestapo. The British authorities felt this made him an unsuitable choice for working in the camp guarding Germans. The incident, in their view, did not require him to resort to firearms and Benke was struck off camp duties until different employment could be found for him.

NOTES

1 Medical inspection and selection of camp site for Italian POWs. The National Archives, Kew. MH 55/1884.
2 R. Douglas Brown, *East Anglia 1944*, Hyperion Books, 1990.
3 *Eastern Daily Press*, Friday 29 January 1943.
4 *Eastern Daily Press*, Wednesday 3 March 1943.
5 After Italy surrendered to Britain, Italian prisoners who volunteered for work were termed 'co-operators' as they were no longer technically the enemy, though they remained POWs.
6 House of Commons Debate, 20 March 1945. Figures reported by Sir J. Grigg.

four

NAZI MURDER ON BRITISH SOIL

MURDER IN SHEFFIELD

'You know today what it is all about. If my fate should not be different, inform my aunt and my mother. I don't mind to go, but only for Germany and the Führer. Do me this favour. Please remember me to all comrades if I have to go.'[1]

So wrote Armin Kuehne, a German POW who, along with Emil Schmittendorf, Heinz Ditzler, Guenter Frenzel, Josef Schneiders and Jurgen Kersting, was accused of killing another prisoner and potentially faced a death sentence. The date was 3 August 1945. In a separate letter to his mother, father, brothers, sisters and aunt, Kuehne wrote:

I have not heard from you since over 1 year. The hour has come now. I have been in captivity since the 8 October 1944 and since the 24 March 1945 I have been accused of murder. On the 7 August my fate will be decided. If I should not be able to return home, don't take it too badly. I have risked my life for my Fatherland, have given my blood for my comrades and I have remained a German and shall remain that to the end. One thing I know, it is only because I am a Nazi and non-Nazis accuse me. They are also Germans. You, my dear parents, must know that I am innocent. I have suffered enough and Manfred had to give his life for Germany, so I can do it as well. My comrades can tell you, dear parents, about my life in captivity. I don't mind to go for you and the liberty of our fatherland.

Kuehne signed his name along with 'Our Führer'. On 13 August he wrote another letter. It was short and blunt:

It has to be. <u>Heil You</u>. <u>Death Sentence.</u>

The series of events that led Kuehne to his death began on 24 March 1945. A fight had broken out in one of the huts. One POW witness named Lange, who resided in the hut, returned from the lavatory to find the fight in progress and the hut in disarray. Everyone was shouting and pushing; Lange managed to push his way down to his bed but the fight was still some way from him. He heard someone shout, 'You are a scoundrel, a traitor!' and someone answered, 'Comrades, let me explain!' Eventually the situation calmed down and those who did not belong to the hut left.

Lange rearranged his bed as it had been disturbed during the scuffle; next to him was Kuehne's bed and that too was a mess. He briefly spotted Kuehne before he left the hut again to go to hut 34. There, too, a fight had started just outside the hut and Lange saw one man badly beaten up. He added that he and others condemned the attack but that there was nothing they could do.

The attack was in response to the British finding an escape tunnel the Germans had been digging. The general opinion in the camp was that someone had let slip the plan. Simply put, they suspected they had a traitor in their midst. Their two main suspects were Huth and Rettig, both non-Nazis which made them instantly traitors in certain POWs' eyes. It was not coincidental that both the tunnel's discovery and the murder took place on 24 March.

Huth and Rettig's political leanings had been discovered by the camp during the general processing of prisoners for repatriation. 'Whites' got special priority over 'blacks', whose ardent Nazism put them at the bottom of the pile for speedy repatriation. It was only shortly after the vetting process when Huth and Rettig were classified as non-Nazis that the murder occurred. It was a mistake on the British camp authorities' part that the two men were not immediately removed from the camp, which was known to have a dangerous element of fervent 'blacks'.

On the same day of the attacks an article was published in the *Wochenpost*, the camp magazine, which many ardent Nazis viewed as British propaganda. Any man receiving the magazine could be marked down as a traitor. Rettig had in fact written the article under 'Uffz G.R.' and it was entitled 'Standard Bearers of the New Age'. He had also written a second article but it was never published.

It was neither Huth nor Rettig who told the British about the tunnel, but rather two other anti-Nazi prisoners; they informed their guard that a tunnel was under construction while they were being moved to camp 6 and were therefore safe from reprisals.

Two of the men accused of murder had also taken part in concocting the escape plan and constructing the tunnel. They were Emil Schmittendorf and Heinz Ditzler. There were a further six men involved with the tunnel's construction, but none had apparently taken part in the attacks. The victim, Rettig, had done nothing to cause the escape plan to be revealed to the British, he was just unfortunate to be in the wrong place at the wrong time.

As it was, the situation might have been even more violent had not Red Cross personnel been within the camp that day. The officials felt the presence of these personnel took some of the force out of the attacks and quelled some of the vengeful thoughts in the men; perhaps this was why Huth survived.

A POW named van Balkom was present shortly after the incident began. He saw Rettig run out of a hut shouting, 'I am innocent'. He was bleeding from his mouth, nose and ears. Several men pursued him, one of which van Balkom thought was Kersting. Rettig ran to the area of the wash houses, but when he got there he appeared groggy and fell down. A crowd was gathering around him and Balkom joined it. He saw Kuehne hit Rettig while he was on the ground. Then the injured man got up and tried to run, but did not get far before he fell again. Someone brought out water and splashed it over his face while someone else kicked him in the head.

Another of the witnesses for the prosecution, a man named Horst Hennemann, gave a clearer picture and was prepared to name Kuehne and Schmittendorf as two of the men he had seen attack Rettig. He was in charge of the wash houses and on the day of the murder he heard a lot of noise and shouting which made him go outside to see what was happening. There was a large pile of coke at the corner of the wash house, about 3ft high, and Hennemann climbed the pile so he could see what was going on.

There was a large crowd and in the centre of it was Kuehne and Schmittendorf; they were facing in Hennemann's direction, about 20m from him, so he could see them clearly. Sitting on the ground a metre from the pair with his back to Hennemann was Rettig. Both Kuehne and Schmittendorf repeatedly punched Rettig in the face; the injured man did not appear to try and protect himself.

The rest of the crowd were standing around watching; Rettig called out to them, 'Comrades, help me!' His plea provoked a lot of shouting and

Hennemann heard someone yell, 'You blackguard, you; you should not call for help!'

Schmittendorf called for someone to bring water out and a man broke from the crowd and fetched a bowl of water from the wash house. Someone threw the water over Rettig and he sank back until he was almost lying on the ground. Schmittendorf hit him again and the rest of the water was poured over him. Almost immediately Rettig sprang to his feet and started to run.

Hennemann headed for the boiler room and from the window he could see the kitchen, dining room, lavatories and a three-sided wall where the rubbish bins usually stood. As he was looking out he saw Rettig run past the window. Three strands of wire ran between the dining room and the kitchen, the top of which had originally been 5ft high, but men had repeatedly climbed over it and now it sagged down. Rettig did not see the wire or misjudged the height; whichever it was, he tripped over it, stumbled a few paces and fell near the space where the rubbish bins were kept, striking his head on the brick wall.

The gang of men, meanwhile, had dispersed when someone called out, 'The Tommies are coming'. Rettig was lying face down on the ground within the rubbish bin area. He was motionless. Hennemann walked past him and into the kitchen. Five minutes later he came out again and Rettig was still lying on the ground, though he had been moved to the path and a German medical man and several orderlies were attending to him.

Georg Bareis was one of the medical orderlies who helped Rettig; he had also seen part of the attack. He had been in his hut when he heard shouting, so he went outside to investigate. The time was about 5.30 p.m. He saw a group of prisoners, estimating their numbers to be between 300 and 500. While he stood there he heard a voice cry out, 'Leave me alone! I am innocent!'

From the sound of the voice Bareis realised the man must be badly injured. He ordered the men to leave him be and back off. The prisoners turned on him and shouted, 'The traitor is trying to help him; beat him up as well!' Bareis retreated to his hut. From the window he saw the prisoners starting to disperse and wander past his hut to the kitchen. Some of the men had clambered onto the kitchen roof and others were being handed a pail of water from a window of the building. Suddenly a cry went up that the Tommies were coming and the men scattered.

Bareis left his hut again. Rettig was lying face down, unconscious. He felt his pulse and decided he must be concussed. Rettig's cheeks were blue-red, the left side of his upper lip was cut through and bleeding; when Bareis checked his pupils they did not react to light. One pupil was the size of a pea while the other had shrunk to a pinhead.

Another POW helped Bareis carry Rettig to the compound's MI room, where they began to loosen his clothes. As Bareis moved Rettig's arm he heard a noise that suggested to him that he had several broken ribs; there was also blood in his mouth, which made Bareis suspect his lungs had been damaged.

Eventually an English officer and two or three soldiers appeared. The officer observed that Rettig's eyes were swollen, there was blood in his mouth and he was having difficulty breathing. A stretcher was organised and Rettig was taken away to the camp hospital. He was still alive when Bareis last saw him.

At the hospital Rettig was seen by Heinrich, the German medical officer. By this time his head and face were badly swollen; the injuries seemed to Heinrich to have been caused by repeated punching and possibly kicking to the head. He suspected Rettig would have a skull fracture or intra-cranial bleeding, so he quickly organised for him to be sent to Wharncliffe hospital by ambulance. Heinrich considered it likely that Rettig would die from his injuries.

British Private Crang was to be Rettig's escort to the hospital. When he first arrived he saw the injured man had been stripped of his clothes and it was clear he had suffered several injuries to his head, face and private parts. Crang sat beside the ambulance driver during the trip to the hospital. There was a sliding panel between the front seats and the body of the ambulance. This was open and Rettig's head was positioned so it was partially through the panel, thus Crang could hear and see what was going on.

Beside Rettig another civilian sat and attended to him. Due to the prisoner's injuries the ambulance driver had instructions to proceed cautiously and slowly. After a few miles Crang heard the patient groan; a short time later the civilian next to Rettig reported he had groaned again, though Crang did not hear him that time.

It took them forty-five minutes to get to the hospital. Rettig was lifted onto a trolley and wheeled into the building where three nurses checked him for signs of life. They reported they could find none. Crang checked for a pulse, heartbeat or breathing, but there was none. Blood was pouring from Rettig's mouth and Crang doubted he could have breathed through that. Another fifteen minutes passed before the doctor arrived and confirmed that Rettig was dead.

Two days after the incident, Hennemann was speaking to Kuehne who told him that Rettig was a blackguard who wrote articles for the *Wochenpost* and had given away the escape tunnel plot. Kuehne said he had taken part in the attack on Rettig and a jagged cut on his hand was the result of the fight.

Kuehne recognised the case against him was growing and started writing letters to potential defence witnesses trying to make it clear what they should say on his behalf:

> Is it not possible for you to testify for me? There are only two points 1). During the beating up I was in the <u>hut</u>. 2). I <u>fetched</u> the rations. If you can testify to this for me I am free. Henneman, Huth and van Balkom accuse me. If you cannot testify for me, I can write 'Finis'. – 6 comrades from Camp 21 have been condemned to death before me, and the same will happen to us. I have told my defending officer:- I gave the signal that the roll call in the hut was finished, then I stood by Hans Fiebig until the crowd came running in after Rettig. Then came the ticket for the rations. I gave it to Fritz and went along to get the rations. Hot and cold. Further, I also repeated the words in which Fritz told Huth to go and they agree. I was in the hut!!!! – If you would testify accordingly, I shall be very grateful. I had no wound on my hand. Am accused of <u>murder</u>.

As a footnote to the letter, Kuehne added: 'Please try by every means, things might go wrong. Please destroy at once after reading. If you can't then <u>remain silent</u>.'

In another letter, one of Kuehne's co-defendants, Emil, wrote to two further witnesses and actually spelled out exactly what they should say on his behalf:

> In case you should have to come down again as witnesses for me, I am writing down for you some points from my statement. Now, I said that immediately after the roll call I went to hut A2 in order to get another palliasse as mine contained too little straw, but the door was nailed up. As I was going back to my own hut I saw a few men, say 20 – 50, running into a hut. I asked what was up and was told in reply that the fellow who had given away the tunnel was in the hut. So I went in too and gave a man, who was already being hit by several people, a few blows with my fist. I also saw that there was a scrap going on on the left. When I turned round, the other lot had gone. So I also went out and found a crowd outside; I went up to it to see what was going on but could not get through the crowd,

so I went along to the left between the hut and the crowd and tried again to see from the other side who was being beaten up, but could not see so went to my hut and put my bed in order. While I was doing this, Hermann came along and asked whether I was coming along for a bath; I replied that I wanted to finish making my bed first and would follow on later. (Here it is most important that you should have seen me in the hut; as far as I am concerned, Hermann followed on a little after Jupp and Ditzler. Jupp may have met me as I was coming in, I had no further conversation with you.) When I made my bed I went for a bath. As I came out of the door I saw a number of men run past the hut; I followed and saw a few men standing by the gate, a man in GAF uniform was standing in the furthest corner, he had his kit with him; I was told that he was the traitor. I went up to him, caught him by the collar, shook him a few times and told him to get out as quickly as possible. Then the sentry came and fetched him out. I went to the latrine, then to have a bath. When I returned to the hut, all except about two had had their meal, but were still sitting at the table. After eating I laid down on my bed. Did not go out again.

Perhaps not convinced his first letter had been clear enough, he wrote to the same witnesses again reiterating his previous statement and adding: 'I went out little during the days before the deed. I made myself slippers of grey material and other things as my shoes were too small. On the day of the deed I wore the slippers as on every other day. I returned from the bath at 7 o'clock.'

Another accused man, Jurgen Kersting, also wrote to an old friend explaining his side of events:

Dear Fritz, I have made the following statement – I hereby state that I did not take part in the beating up in Sheffield camp on 24 March. The proof of this is as follows – After roll-call I went past A1 to the sports ground. Then I went on the sports ground to the exit, that is to say behind all huts. While I moved towards the exit I heard shouting from the camp. Shortly after that I was on the long side of dining room 1, that is near the exit. I could see how a man, whom I did not recognise was carried out on a stretcher by two German prisoners of war and a guard of one English officer and two soldiers. After that I walked down the path which leads from the gate to the Camp Leader's hut. Outside dining room 1 I met a prisoner of war whom I thought I knew. I slapped him on the chest in a friendly way and said, 'I say, where do you come from?' He told me, 'From Westphalia.' I asked him further, 'From which district?' He said to me, 'From the Sauerland.'

I said, 'Now you just tell me you come from Berleburg.' 'Yes,' he said, 'that is right.' Glad to have met there, we then walked together through the camp and parted for the duration of the supper in order to meet again afterwards. We then went for a walk through the camp. When it became dark we went back to E4 where we exchanged snaps of home.

Dear Fritz, this was my statement. I have two witnesses against me. The one thinks it was I who left hut A6 behind Rettig, the other one says that I am supposed to have told him I struck down Rettig near the wash house. Now I am accused of murder. I hope that nothing too much happens to me because none of the other 7 witnesses saw me. If everything goes wrong Fritz, then give my regards to all of them at home, to my homes-town and my beloved forests. Before us 6 men were also sentenced to death for the same thing. Give regards to my mother, my sister and my fiancée. If it comes to this, then I give my life for Germany as my father did. But maybe I shall be lucky here as I was at the front.

The letters were intercepted while the four accused men were being held at the London Cage. There they had been given the job of tea orderlies and a British private named Tylor saw one of the accused running his hand along the bottom of the closed door of room 10. The man was sent back to his room and, along with a second private named Hutton, Tylor opened the door to room 10. Lying on the floor were pieces of paper. The inmates of room 10 denied they were anything to do with them. Hutton took the papers to room 31 where the four accused men resided. He asked one, Ditzler, if these were his documents. He answered that they were supposed to be given to the blonde German in room 10.

During the court proceedings the accused men defended themselves and cross-examined the witnesses. Hennemann was first to relay his story to the court and Schmittendorf was determined to undermine his statements.

'How is it you recognise me so exactly?' he asked.

'By your outward appearance and tall figure,' Hennemann explained.

'Had you ever seen me before?'

'Never.'

Schmittendorf also wanted to know how Hennemann could see so clearly when the crowd was all around, but the answer to that was that Hennemann had been standing on the coke pile. Schmittendorf also tried to insinuate that as Hennemann said he was standing upright the whole time he could not possibly have struck a man who was sitting on the ground, but this was tenuous reasoning at best.

Kuehne tried a similar tactic, suggesting that Hennemann's estimate of the crowd size was wrong; Hennemann stated it was accurate, then Kuehne, like Schmittendorf, wanted to know how Hennemann could have seen them when the crowd was so dense. Again the answer was simple: Hennemann had stood on the coke pile. Eventually, unable to shake the witness from his statement or catch him in a lie, Kuehne sat down. None of the other men wanted to ask Hennemann any questions.

Van Balkom went next, but his story was hazy, as were attempts to cross-examine him; he was merely asked how many men were outside the hut, had anything else unusual happened that day and was the roll call longer than normal. Presumably Kersting and Schneiders, who asked these questions, had something in mind that might exonerate them but they failed to get the answers they wanted from van Balkom.

Next up for the prosecution was a man named Albert Menke; he had only been in the camp since 1 March but shared the same hut as Rettig. On the day of the attack he had been in the wash house when the commotion had started and had gone to the window to see what was happening. He had to stand on tip-toe to see over the crowd and recognised Rettig sitting on the ground with one foot in the drain beneath the rainwater pipe. There was blood on his mouth. Menke noticed Schmittendorf in the crowd and saw him punch Rettig. At that point, however, he went away from the window. He had previously been in a camp in Doncaster with Schmittendorf and had had a disagreement with him that could have led him to a similar fate as Rettig. He was afraid of Schmittendorf.

After his testimony Schmittendorf cross-examined him, though his only question was to clarify about their disagreement at Doncaster. Menke explained that during dinner one day, a group of POWs had approached him and wanted to know what he would say to a British officer if he was asked about the war. Menke had answered that he would say the war was lost. The gang of prisoners called him a blackguard for his answer. Schmittendorf was among them.

Clarification of the argument at Doncaster did nothing to help Schmittendorf's case – if anything it was detrimental, proving that he had previously become angry and aggressive towards prisoners who did not share his views on the war. Menke's statement that he was frightened of what Schmittendorf might do to him should he be seen during the attack on Rettig also added weight to the prosecution's case.

Yet more damning for Schmittendorf was the testimony of a man named Norbert Schulze. He had not witnessed the attack but had heard about it. That same evening he was walking along one of the paths in the camp when he spotted a group of men with Schmittendorf at the centre. The men were cheering Schmittendorf and congratulating him – one said it was good that Rettig had been beaten to death and Schmittendorf replied that the beating-up gang had worked well. He added that the man would not think about treason again.

Someone else in the crowd said Rettig should have been hanged; Schmittendorf concurred but replied that the Red Cross' presence in the camp made that impossible and the beating had been enough. The men repeatedly praised Schmittendorf for his actions and he continually answered that it would have been a lot worse for Rettig if only the Red Cross had not been in the way. At this point Schmittendorf told the men that they must be careful as there might still be traitors in the camp who would give them away. Hearing this Schulze slunk away, not wishing to be recognised by the men.

Again Schmittendorf made a poor attempt to cross-examine the witness, but his only question – which path was it on that you saw me standing with this crowd? – failed to produce an answer that could help his case.

Wilhelm Schulz then began to give evidence. He was one of the few witnesses who had seen the attack almost from the start. He saw Rettig being shoved out of his hut on the night of the attack by three men. His face was covered in blood and his eyes were almost closed. He ran to the corner of the wash house followed by several men, who surrounded him and prevented him from going any further. It was then the large crowd started to form around Rettig and Schulz slipped in among them. He was close to the front and could easily see Schmittendorf beating Rettig, punching him in the head with all his force until Rettig crumpled onto the ground and tried to shield his head with his arm. The crowd was cheering Schmittendorf on and calling out, 'Beat him to death!' and 'Hang him'.

Schmittendorf yanked Rettig's head up by his hair so his arm could no longer protect him. He then kicked him twice in the top of the head, before a cry went round that the 'Tommies were coming' and many of the crowd, including Schulz, left. Surprisingly, Schmittendorf declined to cross-examine Schulz.

Next up was Kurt Isbaner and part of his testimony in the official files has been crossed through in red. Isbaner had been part of the original escape party but when it became clear that he might be implicated in Rettig's death he was quick to give evidence against the accused men. He stated he had met Schneiders on the way from the bath house on the night of the attack and had asked him what was going on earlier that day by the wash house. Schneiders allegedly told him that an uffz (Unteroffizier) had been beaten up, his jaw smashed, his chest crushed and his hair cut because he was a traitor to Germany and had given away the escape tunnel. He went on to say that a short, fair-haired medical soldier had also taken part in the attack and that Rettig should be killed for his treason. Isbaner said he declined to comment and left. It is this entire conversation between Isbaner and Schneiders that has been crossed through in red.

Isbaner continued his testimony. He said that not long after speaking with Schneiders he was back in his hut where Schmittendorf also resided. Schmittendorf was telling others that he had spoken to a German named Huth who denied being a traitor, but that Schmittendorf would account for him later on. The following day, Isbaner interrupted another interesting conversation between the accused Ditzler and Kersting. They were discussing the beating up of Rettig with seven or eight other men, but stopped when Isbaner joined them. Later he heard them begin the conversation again and Kersting announced that he had knocked Rettig down when he first came running out of his hut. A sailor then approached the group and they stopped talking again.

Isbaner seems to have been in the unusual position of having heard the confessions of nearly all the accused men; possibly this is why his testimony was taken with a slight pinch of salt by the authorities.

There was another witness whose evidence was considered even less reliable than Isbaner's. His name was Holtoff, who accused men who had not been named by any of the other witnesses. He did not witness the attack and did not even know about the accusations against the six men until two days after the murder. He was a close friend of Rettig and there were suspicions that they were in a homosexual relationship. His evidence was therefore seen as uncorroborated and probably biased, especially as he was motivated by vague threats supposedly levelled against him after the murder by his former friends. The investigators felt there was little about his testimony they could use.

The seventh witness was Otto Huth. Huth lived in hut A6, which Rettig had been in for about a fortnight; the accused Kersting also lived in that hut. Huth and Rettig were both non-Nazis, a fact that was known in the camp and they were both aware that they were in danger of being beaten up.

Rettig had previously made several written applications to change camps due to the danger he was in. On 24 March, after the British discovery of the escape tunnel, he wrote another application and handed it to a British guard. Rettig and Huth were informed they were to be moved from the camp after evening parade and they duly began packing. Evening parade went by and they returned to their huts to finish packing so they might leave. Rettig left the hut for a moment but immediately came running back in followed by fifteen or twenty men, two of which were Kuehne and Ditzler. These two punched Rettig in the back of his head and neck as he ran away from them. He ran past Huth who turned to find Schmittendorf and Frenzel facing him. Frenzel struck him with his open hand; Schmittendorf punched him in the face and threw him to the ground. Kuehne pulled off the epaulettes from Huth's uniform and others in the crowd started to hit him, one with a stick. Rettig was trapped in a gap between two beds.

After a time the crowd left Huth alone and most of them, including Schmittendorf, began moving to the hut doorway. Schmittendorf aimed a blow at someone but Huth could not see who. Kuehne, Ditzler and Frenzel had also followed the crowd.

The crowd left the hut, leaving Huth alone. A couple of minutes passed before Frenzel and Ditzler suddenly reappeared and spoke briefly to Huth before leaving again. He did not tell the court what they said but must have been aware his life was in serious jeopardy. He waited only a moment before exiting the hut.

Outside he could see Rettig standing by the wash house surrounded by men. Someone was hitting him and another man with his back to Huth was holding half a brick. Huth attempted to slip away between the huts and head for the gates, but ten of the men broke away and chased him. By the time he was in sight of the British guards one of his pursuers had managed to catch hold of his collar.

The guards came to his rescue and Huth was immediately placed in protective custody. He was transferred to the camp sick bay where he saw Rettig being brought in on a stretcher some time later. He was kept in the sick bay for four days before being moved to another camp. No doubt Huth considered he had had a very lucky escape from sharing the same fate as Rettig. None of the men accused opted to cross-examine Huth.

Out of the six men on trial only Kersting and Schneiders chose to give evidence in their defence. Kersting stated that he had been nowhere near the crowd or the attack on Rettig. He added that while walking in the camp he had bumped into another prisoner who he used to know; he had spoken about this man in his letter and went into detail about the conversation they had. This was, however, after Rettig had already been carried away on a stretcher, so the witness, who failed to come forward, could not have provided an alibi anyway.

Schneiders' defence began by saying that he did not have a conversation with Isbaner as the man had suggested, but had been in the bath house with Ditzler and another man. As Isbaner's testimony was the only thing connecting Schneiders to the case, and even then he had made no confession of his involvement during the supposed conversation, Schneiders looked to be pretty much off the hook. He gave no further defence.

Those who investigated the case, though, were less convinced at Schneiders' evidence. His complete denial of being anywhere near the attack was completely opposite to Isbaner's statement, and the investigators felt this was significant, as was his behaviour and bearing during interrogation. But without firmer evidence there was little they could do.

Finally there was the post-mortem evidence from Wharncliffe hospital. Externally most of Rettig's injuries were to his face: his cheeks and eyes were badly swollen, the cartilage of his nose was broken, his lip was cut and bleeding. There were bruises all over his face, worse on the right-hand side. He had also been clearly kicked in the groin. The livid colour of his fingernails, ears and shoulders suggested to the coroner that he had died of asphyxia.

While Rettig had not sustained any fractures to his skull, there was extensive haemorrhaging, with much of the damage on the left side. Surprisingly, despite the violence of the attack, none of the bones in Rettig's face had been broken, nor had he any damage to his tongue or throat. However, there was bile-stained vomit in the air passages and the lungs contained anoxaemic (oxygen-deprived) blood, which went some way to confirming asphyxia. But the pathologist concluded that death had in fact been caused by the severe intra-cranial haemorrhaging resulting from several blows or kicks to the head. While the victim had also suffered from asphyxia due to inhaled vomit, this only sped up his death; without it the pathologist was certain the increasing intra-cranial pressure would have shortly killed Rettig and there was nothing the doctors or surgeons at the hospital could have done.

In the end the court found Kuehne and Schmittendorf guilty of Rettig's murder. They were sentenced to death. In the winter of 1945 they were executed at Pentonville prison, Islington. Armin Kuehne was 21, Emil Schmittendorf was 31.

MURDER AT CAMP 21

There had been a precursor to the murder of Rettig, an incident even more violent that demonstrated the danger faced by 'whites' in a 'black' camp.

As already stated, camp 21 at Comrie, Perthshire, was known for being home to large numbers of ardent Nazis – it was not a location to express anti-Nazi feelings. On 23 December 1944 a rumour went around the camp that there was a traitor in hut 4. His name was Rosterg and he had arrived only the previous day from camp 23 at Devizes.[2]

One witness, Wilhelm Foertsch, was curious to see what was happening in hut 4 and visited the building on his way to the wash houses. What he saw quickly caused him to leave. Rosterg was pinned between two beds being subjected to a mock trial; his chief prosecutors were two German POWs named Koenig and Laise. Koenig was asking Rosterg a question and when the victim failed to answer swiftly enough Koenig hit him across the face with an iron bar wrenched from the boards that held the prisoners' belongings. The scene frightened Foertsch so much that he swiftly left and saw no more of what happened to Rosterg.

Rosterg was not destined to survive that day and twelve men were later charged with his murder. They were Zuehlsdorff, Herzig, Mertens, Goltz, Wunderlich, Brueling, Pallme Koenig, Bienek, Recksiek, Klein, Steffan and Jelinsky. The trouble had begun the day before, as the first witness for the prosecution explained. Fritz Huebner resided in hut 1 and on 22 December four new prisoners arrived in his hut; two of these were Zuehlsdorff and Herzig. During the same evening a conversation began in hut 1 about the *Lagerpost*, the German newspaper the British produced for the camps.

Staunch Nazis held the *Lagerpost* and similar publications, such as the *Wochenpost*, in low regard as propaganda. In fact the papers were purely factual and an attempt by the British to keep their prisoners informed on German home affairs, as well as the progress of the war and British news. This cut little ice with the 'blacks' in the camp and they viewed anyone who received the *Lagerpost* as a traitorous non-Nazi.

During the conversation in hut 1 someone remarked that Rosterg had asked for a copy of the *Lagerpost*. This was met with the comment that if he asked for the paper he could not be a National Socialist. Zuehlsdorff then spoke up: he said he had asked Rosterg if he was a National Socialist and Rosterg had replied: 'No, I am certainly not.'

Rosterg had gone on to say he spoke seven languages and had seen enough of the world to not believe in National Socialism. After this announcement Zuehlsdorff had heard someone say to Rosterg: 'Well, we will see about that.'

Early the next morning another of the accused men, Klein, came to hut 1 and called for Zuehlsdorff and Herzig to follow him to hut 4. Huebner was curious; he had already heard a rumour that there was a traitor in hut 4 so he followed the men. It was between 6 a.m. and 7 a.m., prior to morning roll call. At hut 4 Huebner saw Rosterg standing in front of a stove with a rope noose around his neck. Klein struck Rosterg as he entered, then he turned to the two newest prisoners. 'Is that the swine who arrived with you yesterday?' he asked. They both said yes, despite Rosterg's face being so badly beaten that he was almost unrecognisable.

Koenig was holding the rope, one hand just behind the knot of the noose at the back of Rosterg's neck, and the other holding it a little further back. He told Rosterg, 'Every time you scream swine I'll tighten the rope'. Huebner told the court that it appeared to him that Rosterg could barely groan due to the tightness of the rope, let alone scream.

Bienek stood in front of the victim holding a piece of paper he claimed had been either on Rosterg or in his kit – Huebner could not remember exactly. Bienek read out the paper which said that Rosterg had given away bombing targets and had been responsible for the rounding up of German ATS women by French patriots. Every time Bienek read out one of the statements from the piece of paper Rosterg was supposed to answer the charge, but all he could manage was to groan.

Steffan, Recksiek and Goltz were also present at the 'trial'. Recksiek picked up an iron poker from the stove and hit Rosterg on the cheek and temple with it every time he was supposed to answer one of Bienek's charges. Goltz picked up a square iron bar that was lying in front of the stove and struck Rosterg repeatedly. Finally Steffan, who was the hut leader, stepped forward and announced that he was going to report this to the German camp leader, Sergeant Pirau, and left while the paper was still being read.

A few minutes later Steffan and Pirau returned. Steffan said: 'Stop, stop, we are going to take him to the compound office and the camp leader is here.'

He pushed people aside and Koenig removed the rope from around Rosterg's neck but kept it in his hand. Rosterg was taken to the compound office, Koenig and Goltz following, with a crowd of twenty men, including Huebner, behind them.

At the office Steffan, Pirau, Rosterg and Koenig went inside, the rest of the men waited for them. Only five minutes passed before Koenig reappeared. 'Keep quiet, he has signed a confession and you will have him soon,' he told them, before speaking to Zuehlsdorff, 'and I am making you responsible on your honour as a soldier. You are an SS man and you know what you have got to do.'

Zuehlsdorff agreed and Koenig went back inside. The group of men still waited to see what would happen, Huebner among them. About twenty minutes after Rosterg had first gone in he was suddenly pushed outside by Koenig. The noose was once more around his neck.

'Well, here you are,' Koenig addressed the crowd, 'here is the swine.'

Goltz jumped on Rosterg and pulled him to the ground. He was lying on his back, Goltz kneeling on his chest yanking up the rope around his neck. Several people in the crowd now came forward and began kicking Rosterg all over his body; among them were Zuehlsdorff, Herzig and Mertens. Huebner remained on the sidelines, standing 3 or 4ft away from Rosterg's thigh.

Suddenly someone in the crowd starting calling out, 'Hang him up, hang him up!' And Rosterg's tormentors began to drag him towards the lavatories. Goltz, Herzig and Zuehlsdorff grabbed the rope and used it to pull Rosterg, who was apparently now unconscious, on his side across the ground.

Huebner followed behind the procession; it was not very far to the lavatories but they had to cross a raised stone path which interrupted their progress while Rosterg's body was hauled up and over. By now around 100 POWs had gathered and were watching what was happening. Rosterg was dragged through the crowd, Huebner no more than 7ft behind him.

At the lavatories the doorway proved another obstacle as it was only wide enough for two men. Goltz and Zuehlsdorff dragged him through and Mertens and Herzig came behind. Huebner followed too and stood behind the partition that spilt up the lavatories – it was not very tall so he was able to see over it. Several other prisoners also gathered inside until the building was quite crowded.

Goltz and Zuehlsdorff put the end of the rope over the pipe. Mertens attempted to pull on the end and lift up Rosterg's body, but it was too heavy, so he called to the others to lift Rosterg up. Herzig and Zuehlsdorff lifted the body up and Goltz tied the rope around the pipe; as soon as the rope was tight they ran away. Rosterg was left hanging with his toes 6in off the floor. He appeared unconscious to Huebner, who left the lavatories and returned to his hut.

At 8.30 a.m. the morning roll call commenced. Afterwards Koenig found Huebner and told him to come to hut 4. Waiting for him there were Klein, Bienek and a sergeant who he did not know. Koenig asked him if he had seen the men who were there when Rosterg hung himself. Huebner answered that he had. Koenig then warned him that he would suffer the same fate if he told anyone what had happened. Huebner returned to his hut.

Zuehlsdorff was the first to cross-examine Huebner. He wanted to know if Huebner was certain that it was Rosterg's name he had mentioned during the conversation prior to Rosterg's death. Huebner was adamant it was. Then Zuehlsdorff suggested that Koenig had not been talking to him when he instructed the 'SS man' to deal with Rosterg, but Huebner was not to be swayed – he knew it was Zuehlsdorff who had been given the order.

Next Herzig spoke up, but his questions did not go beyond asking Huebner what clothes Herzig was wearing that day.

Then Goltz stood. 'Couldn't you have made a mistake in identifying me as the man who fixed the rope round the pipe?' he asked.

'No, there is no mistake. I recognise you.'

'Is it not a figment of your imagination that in hut 4 I hit Rosterg with an iron bar and followed him to the compound office?'

'I am not mistaken. I do not know why I should say something about someone whom I have never seen before unless I saw it happen.'

'If I bring witnesses that I have not hit him, would you still be certain?'

'My statement remains, it is the whole truth.'

Brueling then stood. However, his questioning clearly showed he had not listened to Huebner's testimony and in fact went some way to incriminating himself. Huebner had made no mention of Brueling, yet Brueling asked him if he could have been mistaken in saying he had tied the rope to the pipe in the lavatory. As Huebner had made no mention of Brueling he was clearly perplexed by the question and answered that he was certain Goltz had tied the rope, but added that Brueling may have been there.

Now Pallme Koenig stood. He wanted to know if Huebner was certain he was in hut 4. Huebner was certain and he now added to his testimony saying it was Koenig who, when the trial was interrupted, took Rosterg screaming to the wash house and washed the blood from his face before bringing him back to the hut to continue the trial. He was also adamant that Koenig had been the one who carried the rope to the compound office.

Koenig's questioning revealed a piece of intriguing information: 'Did you have a talk with me on the 23rd, and on that day did you know me?'

'I knew you because you used to come to my hut and you used to say that there was something fishy about me and you tried to find out about me.'

Bienek was up next and asked a clever question that must have been in everyone's minds: 'Why, as you were present during the whole of this affair, did you not fetch any help?'

Huebner's reply was simple: 'Because the whole hut was surrounded by people, some of whom had knives and were watching for anyone who might go to get help.'

'Could you not have got to any guard who was outside the wire?'

'That was not possible.'

Recksiek stood and only asked if Huebner was certain he had hit Rosterg. Huebner answered yes. Klein began his questioning, wanting to know if Huebner had witnessed the whole assault and, more puzzling, whether he had eaten breakfast that morning which Huebner denied. The last to ask a question was Jelinsky who only wanted to know how Huebner recognised him. The other defendants declined to cross-examine the witness.

The next prosecution witness was Hermann Bultmann, who had arrived in the same draft of prisoners as Rosterg on 22 December. He last spoke to Rosterg at 9 p.m. on the night before his murder. On the morning of 23 December Bultmann and several other men were roused from their beds by a naval officer, who told them to get dressed and follow him. There was no reason given for his order.

The naval officer was named Walproel and he only ordered those men who had just come from the Devizes camp to dress and follow him. Seven men accompanied Bultmann, among them Wunderlich and Goltz; they were all taken to hut 4 where a crowd of men was gathering. Rosterg was inside standing by his bed, his face and lips were badly swollen and blood was weeping from one eye. A man stood in front of him, who Bultmann thought was Pallme Koenig. The noose was already around Rosterg's neck and the tail end of the rope was wrapped around his throat as well.

In Bultmann's opinion it seemed that Recksiek was in charge of the proceedings. At this point the crowd started shouting and accusing Bultmann of being a traitor as well. Frightened that he too might be beaten up if the mob of Germans turned, Bultmann pushed his way through to Steffan, the hut leader, and asked what he was accused of, adamantly stating that he was not a traitor. Steffan asked if he had been a member of the Hitler Youth movement. Thinking on his feet, Bultmann answered yes, even though that was a lie.

Attention now slipped from Bultmann as Bienek had appeared with a slip of paper. It was said the paper had been found on Rosterg and Bienek was translating bits of it and reading them out. Bultmann believed the paper was from Rosterg's record from the previous camp. Meanwhile, a yellow file was being handed around the massed men. Bultmann saw the file and recognised Wunderlich's name written on the inside cover; there were other lists in the file of prisoners who had been at the Devizes camp.

One of the ringleaders of the mock trial told the crowd that the lists of names were those of Nazis who were to be handed to the British. Rosterg had supposedly gathered these names, further proving his traitorous activities. Bultmann knew otherwise. Rosterg had been an interpreter, clerk and compound sergeant at their previous camp which meant he dealt with lots of paperwork; the lists were in fact the names of men assigned to the delousing squads and similar things. The file was a perfectly innocent series of administrative lists.

During the reading of the lists many men were striking Rosterg with their fists, and when Wunderlich read his name in the file he attacked him also, hitting him on the face and chest until he was held back by the crowd. By this point Rosterg had been dragged from between the bunks and was now in front of the stove with Pallme Koenig hovering over him. Someone was shouting for Rosterg to be left alone as he had had enough. Bultmann was trying to edge away through the crowd to the doorway, but was intercepted. He was taken to the lavatory then back to his hut where, almost immediately, he was summoned again by a naval officer and taken to the compound office.

Inside the office, Rosterg, Pallme Koenig, Steffan and the compound leader Pirau were already assembled. Two German clerks had been roused from their sleep and were hastily getting dressed. Everyone in the office now started questioning Bultmann about his record. Rosterg was stood to one side, so badly knocked about that he was barely aware of the proceedings. At one point Koenig grabbed him by his shirt and shouted at him to stand to attention when being questioned.

Bultmann did not tell the court what questions were asked or what thoughts were crossing his mind during the interrogation, but no doubt he was afraid and well aware that Rosterg's fate could easily be his own.

After a time, Bienek appeared with the piece of paper and again started reading out extracts. The effect of this was to imply that Rosterg had given away ATS girls to the French patriots and also the positions of petrol dumps and factories. During the reading Koenig struck Rosterg in the face again for not standing to attention properly.

Finally, much to Bultmann's relief no doubt, he was instructed to leave the office and was escorted back to his barracks. Yet only a few minutes later he and all the other men from Devizes were once again summoned. They returned to the compound office in time to see Koenig come out of the door and declare: 'This swine is going to hang himself and if he doesn't, you bloody well know what to do!' Pallme Koenig then turned his attention on Bultmann and said, 'And I want to see that this tall fellow here (meaning me [Bultmann]) is a proper National Socialist and takes part in it.'

Then Rosterg was forcefully pushed out of the door, stumbled and began to squeal. Goltz leapt forward and dragged him to the ground by the rope that was once again around his neck. The crowd was kicking Rosterg as he collapsed to the ground; Goltz knelt astride him and with one hand pulled the noose tight, while with the other he pulled up the rope, effectively throttling Rosterg. Up until this point Rosterg had still been squealing, but now he went silent.

Bultmann witnessed men stamping on Rosterg's head, face and body. The assault endured for another minute, and then several men snatched up the rope and started dragging Rosterg across the ground. Bultmann was pushed ahead by the crowd, while Rosterg was dragged behind him. They arrived at the lavatories and a cry that a guard was coming meant Rosterg was hastily dragged inside. It is unclear at this point whether Rosterg was still alive, but if he was at least he was mercifully unconscious.

Several men now took part in lifting Rosterg's body so the rope could be tied to the pipe. Bultmann stood by the lavatory exit, behind the body. He saw Zuehlsdorff, Wunderlich and Goltz all present at the hanging. As soon as it was over Bultmann, who probably still wondered if Koenig had intentions to do the same to him, hurried back to his hut. Later on he heard Goltz boast how he had pulled the rope tight and Brueling remarked that he needed to go to the wash house because he had stamped on Rosterg and now his boots were full of blood. Bultmann looked at his boots and saw that they were indeed covered with blood from the toecap up to the laces.

After his testimony Goltz was the first to stand and cross-examine Bultmann. He tried to imply that Bultmann had had a hand in stringing up Rosterg, but he denied this. Next Brueling stood and deepened the hole he had already begun to dig for himself. He had hardly been mentioned by Bultmann and certainly it had not been said that he had taken part in the hanging, yet Brueling effectively confessed to taking part by asking Bultmann if he did not help him to drag Rosterg by the rope. Bultmann denied pulling the rope, but said that he thought it was Brueling who had pushed him into the lavatory.

Pallme Koenig stood next. His intent was to make it seem like he had interceded on Rosterg's behalf. He asked Bultmann if he had not heard someone shout to leave Rosterg alone and hand him over to the British, and if that same someone had tried to hold back the crowd. It appears Koenig was trying to improve his case but Bultmann simply answered that he heard the cry but had not seen who called out.

Koenig then wanted to know if Bultmann had carried out German orders given to him while he was a POW. Bultmann's answer was bitter: 'So far as the person who gives the orders has authority and so far as the orders do not conflict with morals and decency, but nowadays the situation is such that one must be ashamed to be a German.'

Bienek then stood and wanted to clarify that he had not accused Rosterg of any traitorous crimes, but only read out statements from the piece of paper. Bultmann told him that what he had read out clearly led to Rosterg's accusation. Bienek repeated that he had made no accusations, only read from the paper. Bultmann snapped at him: 'You have always been inciting and called him lots of names.'

Recksiek began his questioning with the peculiar question, 'Did I at that time wear a beard?' presumably to throw doubt on Bultmann's identification of him. Bultmann answered that he could not remember.

Finally it was Klein's turn and his questioning revealed some new information; for a start it seemed that Bultmann had been told that he was to leave the camp again on 23 December. This may suggest that the British staff were aware that there could be trouble and were attempting to remove anyone who could be in danger. Klein then pursued an intriguing line of questioning. He first wanted to know if Bultmann remembered him saying to him: 'I told you that Rosterg had betrayed you and that he was a traitor and that you were a traitor.'

Bultmann answered: 'I now remember that somebody ... accused me of being a traitor and asked Rosterg if I was a member of his clique and he said "no".'

How this actually helped Klein's case is unclear.

The third witness to present evidence was a Waffen SS man named Lergenmueller. His main testimony was not that he had witnessed the assault but that two or three weeks after the murder he had discovered that Brueling, who he had previously known, was in the camp. He went to visit him and they talked about a lot of things, including Rosterg's death. Brueling boasted that he had taken part in the killing of Rosterg and that they had done it because Rosterg had given away an escape attempt at the Devizes camp.

The only one to question Lergenmueller from among the accused was Klein, who only did so to confirm the man's rank and position in the German army.

The fourth witness was a man named Wilhelm Schmidt. Schmidt shared a hut with Zuehlsdorff and Herzig. On the morning of the murder he went to the dining hall for breakfast; normally he sat on the same table as Zuehlsdorff but he was absent. While eating he heard the shouts of a man as if he was being hurt. Schmidt went out to investigate and found a crowd of ten men outside the wash house and more men inside. He asked what was happening but did not report what answer he received, then he returned to the dining hall, finished his breakfast and went to his hut.

A short time later he was due at the kitchen and set out for it. His route took him past the compound office, where a lot of men had gathered. He paused and saw the German camp leader Claas enter the office and close the door behind him. The crowd were shouting out 'criminal' and 'traitor'. Schmidt was apparently curious and went up to the office and opened the door a fraction so he could see inside. There he saw Rosterg, his face covered in blood, and various men, including Steffan, Pirau and Pallme Koenig, standing in the room with him.

After glimpsing inside, Schmidt closed the door again. He headed in the direction of the kitchen but turned around when he got there and returned to the compound office. He did this several times until he saw Pallme Koenig appear. Koenig shouted at the crowd: 'You had better keep quiet so that the sentries will not hear!' He added: 'I will hand him over to you soon.'

Schimdt then told of the end of the assault and Rosterg's hanging, his story consistent with what had previously been said. He added that when Mertens was trying to tie Rosterg up he asked Schmidt to help him, but he refused.

Zuehlsdorff was first to cross-examine Schmidt, wanting to know if he had perhaps muddled him up for someone else, but Schmidt denied this. He was then asked: 'While Rosterg was being murdered did you feel pity for him?'

'I thought all the time, how can these people kill a person? – I couldn't have done a thing like that.'

Zuehlsdorff then suggested that Schmidt had in fact called Rosterg a swine after the murder and said he deserved to die. Schmidt answered:

That is not true. At a later date when the camp leader read out a document that was supposed to be a copy of Rosterg's statement I said that if a man had done that it was not very nice but that we as prisoners of war had no authority to deal with the matter. Those in Germany ought to deal with it. I only said this because anybody who expressed views contrary to National Socialism would have suffered Rosterg's fate or been beaten up.

Herzig then tried to imply that he too had been misidentified by the witness. Schmidt was vague in denying this. Mertens pursued a similar line; Schmidt admitted that at the time it was not quite dawn and still relatively dark, but was certain it was Mertens who had asked him to lend a hand when stringing up Rosterg.

Mertens also wanted to know why Schmidt had not gone for help. The witness confessed he had not thought about it at the time and had later learned that anyone who might have attempted to get help for Rosterg would have been clubbed to death with iron bars, especially by men from the Afrika Corps in hut 6.

When Goltz cross-examined him it turned out that Schmidt was another prisoner who was hoping to ask the authorities to move him to a different camp because he felt vulnerable. This seems to have been the general atmosphere at the camp, that anyone who was not an ardent Nazi lived with a pall of dread and fear hanging over them.

Pallme Koenig, Jelinsky and Bienek also tried to imply that Schmidt could not possibly have clearly recognised them as the morning was so dark. Recksiek only wanted to know how Schmidt knew his name. Klein stumbled into a similar dilemma as Brueling by asking Schmidt to confirm he had been in the lavatories where Rosterg was hanged wearing his POW uniform. Schmidt answered that he had not seen him that morning, meaning Klein had effectively placed himself at the scene.

Steffan's questioning revealed the level of paranoia and fear that had built up in the camp. Prisoners could send messages to the British camp staff by placing them in a mailbox between two huts; when explaining why he had not used this system, Schmidt said the box was always being watched and he could have been suspected if he had attempted to post a message. Steffan asked did he not know that compound leader Pirau had made it clear that POWs could use the box without concern. Schmidt said he had heard no such statement. He added that he wanted to leave the camp, along with several other men, but that this had become known to other prisoners and they had summoned Schmidt and the others to a hut on 25 January. During the discussion about them leaving one of their number was badly beaten up.

The fifth witness for the prosecution was a British captain from the Intelligence Corps. His name was not identified in the records, but he had taken the statements of Zuehlsdorff, Mertens, Goltz, Wunderlich and Brueling. He had also taken a statement from Steffan prior to that POW being arrested with the others. His testimony was not questioned by the prisoners present.

The sixth witness was Klaus Merfield, who had been on coal fatigue on the day of the murder. Schmidt was also due to be on coal fatigue that day, which was why he had been heading for the kitchen when he spotted the crowd outside the compound office. While sorting the coal, Merfield heard noises coming from the wash house and went to investigate. He saw Rosterg inside with a rope around his neck, with several other men crowded around. One German, who he thought had been Pallme Koenig, was holding the rope in such a way that he could twist it to tighten it around the unfortunate Rosterg's neck. Merfield heard him warn Rosterg that if he screamed he would twist the rope tighter. At that point Merfield left.

Later he went with Schmidt to the lavatories and witnessed the hanging of Rosterg. He corroborated that Mertens had asked Schmidt to help him with the rope, but Schmidt had refused and the two men had returned to the kitchens.

Zuehlsdorff, in his cross-examination, returned to the question about whether Merfield had had breakfast that day, presumably trying to find a witness to say he had been in the dining hall at the time of the murder. Merfield was of no help as he had not eaten breakfast. Herzig also tried and failed to establish he was in a different hut at the time of the assault.

Mertens, who had been specifically named by Merfield, attempted to put doubt on the witness' ability to see him when the lavatory was so crowded with men. Merfield, however, answered by saying he had asked Schmidt to move over so he could see and then raised himself up on Schmidt's shoulders, which gave him a clear view of Mertens.

Goltz asked Merfield why he had not gone for help when he saw Rosterg being assaulted. He answered that he did not know Rosterg and that it was fairly commonplace for men who had been caught stealing to be taken to the wash house and dealt with. He assumed that this was what was happening to Rosterg and that he would be let go eventually.

Pallme Koenig and Bienek both asked if Merfield had spoken about the Rosterg murder with the other witnesses. Merfield said he had while they were being held in London before the trial.

Next to give evidence was Rudolf Vollstaedt, one of the clerks who had been in the office during Rosterg's interrogation. Vollstaedt explained that when Rosterg was brought in by the German compound officer Pirau, he was covered in blood. The second clerk Bretschmeider and the camp interpreter, who also slept in the compound office, quickly left, leaving Vollstaedt alone. He got on with dressing and making his bed and claimed he did not hear what was being said to Rosterg.

After five minutes everyone left the room except for Rosterg. Within a matter of seconds Pallme Koenig burst back in, grabbed Rosterg by his shirt and accused him of being a traitor. He told Rosterg that he had many thousand Germans on his conscience. Rosterg denied that he had done anything; another man who had come in sneered at this response and punched him in the head.

Pallme Koenig then told Rosterg that if he had any honour left, he would go and hang himself. Rosterg replied that he could not do such a thing. Koenig then told him to get out. Rosterg left, the rope still around his neck, but perhaps hopeful that the ordeal might be over. It was not to be; Pallme Koenig followed him outside while Vollstaedt remained quietly in the office.

Otto von Coll presented his testimony next. He slept in hut 5 and on the night before the murder he heard people shouting 'swine' and 'traitor' in hut 4. He thought he also heard someone whining before loud singing suddenly began.

The next morning von Coll went to hut 4 and witnessed Rosterg's mock trial. The victim's face was unrecognisable, being so swollen and bloodied, and spots of blood stained the front of his tunic. Von Coll was present until Rosterg was taken to the compound office, then he went to eat his breakfast. A short time later he was walking back to hut 5 and passing hut 4 when he heard Klein shout out from inside: 'Now he hangs.' Along with several other people, Bienek included, von Coll went to the lavatory and saw Rosterg hanging there. He stated that Bienek had said it was a shame that Rosterg was hanged and that it should have been dealt with differently, but this piece of testimony has been crossed out in the records with red pencil.

Von Coll also claimed that in February 1945 he was transferred to camp 23 at Devizes. There he met with Jelinsky and they began talking about the murder. Jelinsky said he had stamped on Rosterg's face with his boots. Von Coll asked what he would do if his involvement in the murder was found out. Jelinsky replied that he would die for his führer. This last statement also has a faint red pencil mark crossing through it, leading to the assumption that the British did not entirely believe in von Coll's truthfulness.

Goltz and Wunderlich in their cross-examination wanted to know if von Coll could remember details such as the colour of Rosterg's uniform and his epaulettes. Pallme Koenig, on the other hand, was trying to build up his defence case. He wanted to know if the crowd von Coll had seen were full of anger and hate. Von Coll answered yes. Then Pallme Koenig wanted to know if von Coll had seen him tighten the rope around Rosterg's neck or hit him. Von Coll answered he had not, but that he had heard Koenig repeatedly say to Rosterg, 'Did you do that, you swine?'

Koenig was attempting to prove that, rather than being an attacker, he was in fact Rosterg's saviour. He wanted to know if von Coll had witnessed him protecting Rosterg from the crowd when he was taken to the compound office. Von Coll answered that, yes, he had seen that, but then Koenig's facade of being Rosterg's protector crumbled with one question. He asked if von Coll had heard him tell the crowd to hit Rosterg. No, von Coll answered, presumably to Koenig's delight, but he went on to add that while Pallme Koenig said nothing directly, every time he asked Rosterg a question he gestured with his head to men standing behind and they struck Rosterg. This happened every time Koenig made the movement with his head and von Coll was certain this was a silent signal.

Bienek was also building his defence, trying to indicate that all he did was read out a bit of paper that was in English, translating it into German. Von Coll acknowledged that he had seen Bienek ask other men in the room the meaning of certain words on the paper and that he was trying to be as accurate as he could with his translation.

Finally it was the turn of the accused men to give evidence, most of whom declined, but Herzig, Recksiek and Jelinsky were prepared to stand up and speak out.

Herzig said that he had been part of the group of new arrivals that came to Comrie on 22 December. On 23 December he, along with the other new prisoners, was ordered to come to hut 4. Inside the hut was a large crowd. Herzig and some of the other men were asked questions about their recent arrival; Bultmann came later and he too was asked questions but Herzig could not remember what they were. The crowd was murmuring about there being a traitor and someone was reading from a piece of paper, but Herzig could neither hear what he was saying nor identify the reader. Then someone was led from the hut, but Herzig didn't see who it was either and returned to his barracks. Later he learned someone had been hanged. Herzig's defence was the age-old plea that he heard nothing, saw nothing and did nothing.

Recksiek simply stated that he neither touched, struck nor did anything that led to the death of Rosterg. His evidence is crossed through in red.

Jelinsky claimed that the first he knew about Rosterg was when he was told someone had hanged themselves in the lavatories. He went to look and saw a man covered in blood hanging from a pipe. Later on, when he was sitting in his hut with several other men, he learned more details and the reasons behind Rosterg being attacked. He also learned that he had not hung himself. Jelinsky said that he told the other men that what Rosterg's attackers did was wrong and that treason was a matter to be dealt with by the German people's court. He explained that after this statement he was ostracised for a long time by the other men.

But Jelinsky had a lot to say about Otto von Coll, including the honesty of his statements. Jelinsky claimed that after he had criticised the assault on Rosterg he too came under suspicion for being a stool pigeon, and rumours quickly spread that he actually originated from France. Von Coll, he said, gathered these rumours. Von Coll was suspected of being a super-Nazi, especially when collections were being taken in the camp for the führer's birthday. Von Coll donated the extraordinary sum of 25,000 marks from his account in Germany. It was also rumoured that he had lied about his father being a diplomat on the staff of Herr von Papen.

Jelinsky explained that after von Coll had collected this slander against him, he had approached Jelinsky and told him he had written everything down and was going to report him to the Gestapo when they returned to Germany.

Von Coll and Jelinsky were both medical students and the only time they spoke was during lectures within the camp, and their conversation always revolved around Jelinsky's supposed treachery. In February 1945 all POW medical students were sent to camp 16 to continue their training. Jelinsky was glad to be there as many of his old comrades were in the camp and he was well known. One day he was standing on the main road with several men, including von Coll, and Jelinsky was telling them about the hanging of Rosterg at camp 21. But, he adamantly stated, he said nothing about taking part in the attack, either kicking, beating or hanging Rosterg, and that, as far as he could remember, was the only time he spoke with von Coll on the subject.

Jelinsky and von Coll were then moved to camp 186, where Jelinsky was given a tent to share with seven other men. The men formed a unit under the command of Jelinsky, entitled Battle-Group X or Battle-Group Jelinski. The intention of the unit was to stand up against Marxism which prevailed in camp 186, and for the group to prove themselves 'decent German front-soldiers by our bearing, attitude and political views'.

In particular, Battle-Group X maintained the German Nazi salute even though the majority of the camp had switched to a non-political salute of touching the cap. Von Coll was part of the group and, in Jelinsky's view, had become highly active in standing up against Marxism, going so far as to rip written orders down from the camp notice boards, including the official army communiqués and notices from the camp leader to not use the German salute. Jelinsky explained that this was not an order from him and that he had even, along with another Battle-Group X member, restrained von Coll when he had attempted to tear down new army communiqués. Jelinksy had told him that he could write in blue pencil on the notices 'Careful Enemy Propaganda', but that he had no right to tear them down.

After only a week von Coll and Jelinsky were on the move again, this time to camp 23 where an academy was being set up for medical students. Von Coll now fell in with a group of anti-Nazis; when Jelinsky asked him about this he explained that he, 'as a diplomat, has to keep in well with both sides'. Jelinsky was disgusted and informed von Coll that he would remain a German soldier until the last Bolshevist was driven from Europe. Von Coll, however, kept in with the anti-Nazis, receiving bread and cigarettes from them and even, at least on the surface, becoming a fanatical anti-Nazi. This did not surprise Jelinsky, who told the court: 'Coll is bound to be where there is a chance to make a little bit on the side.'

Von Coll now began to turn on Jelinsky at camp 23; he called him 'his most redoubtable political enemy and he would not rest until [Jelinsky] would kneel in chains before him in London'. While in his hut von Coll was also supposed to have said that his happiest day would be when he could wade through Nazi blood up to his knees. Jelinsky claimed that when von Coll said this he got into hysterics and began frothing at the mouth, but he had only heard this from other people and not witnessed it himself.

At Easter, von Coll approached him and informed him that he was now a sub-lieutenant in the 'Free Germany' movement and that Jelinsky was recognised as the leader of the Nazis within the camp. He added that Jelinsky's only chance was to radically change his political views and join the 'Free Germany' movement. Jelinsky was disgusted by this offer and walked off. After that time he refused to talk to von Coll.

THIRSTY GERMAN PRISONERS IN THEIR BARBED WIRE CAGE
OFFICIAL PHOTOGRAPH. CROWN COPYRIGHT RESERVED

1. Prior to the Geneva Convention there were fewer regulations on how POWs should be treated. Camps were often basic with limited resources. These men have just been brought in and rush to the water tanks to quench their thirst. (*All images are author's collection unless otherwise stated*)

2. Despondent German soldiers, captured during fighting in Reichswald in 1945, are guarded by an armed British soldier. These men will now be sent to a nearby camp and then transported to England.

3. Once the men stopped fighting, despair over their capture could sink in. While one German at the back smokes, two of his comrades hang their heads. This picture was taken near Goch.

4. *Above*: This soldier, being transported back from the front presumably, is clearly injured and is escorted by medical personnel.

5. *Right*: These girls appear to be nurses about to board a train. Whether they are headed for the front or a military hospital remains a mystery.

6. This unusual German photo shows several officers around field maps presumably deciding their next move. Information about military tactics and plans was something the British were always looking for when interrogating prisoners.

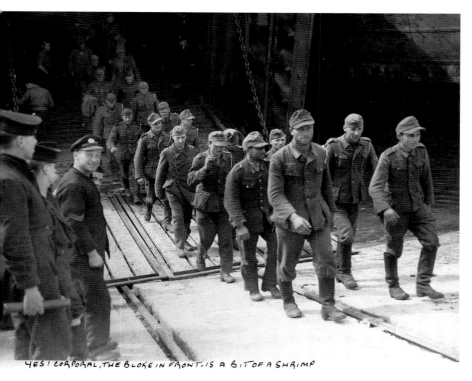

YES! CORPORAL, THE BLOKE IN FRONT IS A BIT OF A SHRIMP

7. Here 300 German prisoners disembark at a British port from a tank landing craft. The comment written at the bottom of the picture is possibly referring to the young boy at the front, far right.

8. A group of newly arrived Germans survey their surroundings. A sewn-on 'P', signifying 'prisoner', can be seen on the man on the left's coat arm.

9. Another party of German prisoners march through British docks, observed by an off-duty British soldier and his sweetheart; the smiles on these men's faces show most were not unhappy to be in England.

10. Though they were the enemy, many women couldn't resist making contact with the German prisoners and this eventually led to several German–British marriages.

11. It was sometimes easy to forget that most men had families at home who were worried about them. This officer stands in front of a farm building, presumably with his children.

12. German troops line up for an informal photocall.

13. Camps liked to be self-sufficient as much as possible and most prisoners were given jobs around the site to keep them occupied. This picture, taken in 1939 in the north of England, shows some of the earliest POWs digging over grassland which will become a vegetable plot.

14. In the camps, teams of prisoners would work in the kitchens and canteen serving their comrades food. This large group of canteen staff are clearly enjoying posing for a picture.

15. Clandestine meetings within the camp confines had to be performed under the cover of night. These would mostly be to do with organising escapes, April 1944.

16. Camp life need not be dull. Here several Germans have dressed up and have formed an impromptu band.

17. Rebuilding London was a large-scale project in which many prisoners were involved. These two are shovelling dirt on a site at Shooter's Hill, London, ready for a new housing estate.

18. Another group at Shooter's Hill are digging out a trench which may be for pipes, 22 May 1945.

19. This German POW, Ernest, was working in Ashford, Kent, in 1947. After the war, Britain was short of a labour force and many prisoners were kept back to assist with harvesting.

20. Another picture of Ernest, this time with some fellow POWs, who all appear to have been working on a farm.

21. Unusually, one German POW wears his military uniform while the other, Ernest, wears civilian clothes, when clearly they are outside the camp. It is 1943 so Ernest was clearly destined to remain in England for at least the next four years (see plate 19).

22. British farmers appreciated having men on their farms who knew about handling and caring for horses.

23. This picture shows a group of Germans listening to a lecture at Wilton Park, Beaconsfield – an educational camp that became known as the 'POW University'.

24. This group of probably Italian prisoners march off a hospital ship in April 1943. The Italians were only too glad to be out of the war, hence the smiles.

25. More prisoners happily walk into Britain, one having to juggle a crutch and walking stick. Judging by the date (April 1943) and their appearance they are probably Italians.

26. In what is quite clearly a staged photograph, Italian POWs working on a farm gather round a military guard who translates their instructions for the day from English to Italian using a dictionary.

27. It was not only British work that kept the men busy; this magnificent chapel was in fact created from a POW camp Nissen hut. It was decorated by very talented Italian prisoners. (*With kind permission of Mike Carden*)

28. Wartime Europe was far from a pleasant place to live; the destruction of homes, mass evacuations and the threat of invasion often left property abandoned. Is this group of Germans helping with the furniture or looting it? Only the photographer could tell us.

29. German families felt pride in their sons and husbands fighting for their country, even if they did not agree with the Nazi regime.

30. When repatriation began it was the wounded and those unfit for work who were first to be shipped home.

31. Wounded and clearly suffering the after-effects of battle, these men regroup and treat their injured.

32. Many Germans wondered just what they would be returning to after repatriation; so much of their country had been destroyed, just like this bridge, clearly hit by a bomb.

33. So many lives were lost during the war and survivors could often feel guilty that they had lived when their comrades had died. There is no indication where this rudimentary cemetery is.

34. While most of the POW camps are long vanished beneath the soil, and in some cases new housing estates, the prisoners did leave some mementoes behind other than just memories. The Italian Chapel on Orkney is just such an example. (*With kind permission of Mike Carden*)

A short time later Jelinsky was hospitalised due to an attack of malaria. When he returned to the camp a fortnight later he discovered von Coll had left, but before he had gone he had spread a rumour around the camp stating that Jelinsky was a murderer. He claimed that von Coll had done this so that Jelinsky's reputation and political position was ruined. Aside from his medical duties, Jelinsky was intent on combating Marxism in the camp; with Coll spreading rumours about him, he found this impossible.

Jelinsky was so furious that he went to the German camp leader who promised to quash the rumours. He also approached some of the camp doctors who supposedly told him that von Coll was a 'harmless lunatic' who spread 'silly lies' to get attention for himself and that anyone could see this. Jelinsky inferred that von Coll suffered from hallucinations, was a prolific liar and that all he had said in the trial was simply to garner importance for himself.

Jelinsky's evidence, like von Coll's relating to him, is crossed through in red and it seems likely that the court decided there was too much antagonism between the two men for either man's statement to be taken as the full truth.

Koenig was apparently satisfied with the defence he had provided and certain that he would not be convicted of the murder; he wrote to the lieutenant-colonel who had advised him on his defence, talking confidently about his future plans:

> After the end of our trial and most likely our stay here, I should like in the name of my comrades and in my own name, to express to you, sir, our gratitude. Due to your advice we asked for British officers to be assigned to us for our defence and we have been agreeably surprised. Without your advice we would, most likely, have made a different choice.
>
> Due to your and the major's instructions, our stay here has been alleviated, we were allowed to work and time passed relatively quickly.
>
> I beg to be allowed to ask you a favour. When we are being sent away from here, we would be grateful to you, sir, if we were not sent to a camp where we would have to wait from one empty day to another, but could help to rebuild the destroyed parts of London.
>
> If it should not be possible for us to work together, I beg to ask to be transferred to an Austrian PW camp.
>
> I beg to let me tell you this myself and to be convinced that even after our return to our homes we shall be pleased to remember your personality, sir, and that of the major.

Bienek, however, was less optimistic. A note was discovered on him during September; it seemed he was intending to try and pass it to some of the other accused men. He wrote:

> The prosecutor has demanded the death penalty against our six comrades ... The verdict has not yet been promulgated but it is not likely to be very mild ... I cannot understand at all why Herzig has not been acquitted too, as he is completely innocent!!! ... Sk. [Skrupke?] is to be my defending counsel. In his opinion they can't tie anything on me, if there is even a shadow of justice ... As I now live on the floor below yours we could establish an 'air mail' with thread during fog and darkness. No. 10 has three windows. In front of the centre window and the one on the left is a balcony. The centre window is about 1½ metres to the right (south) of the lamp-standard. This is so that you will know out of which window to lower the 'air mail' so it will dangle in front of the centre window ... Wunderlich can take the biggest risks as we do not need him as a witness and, after all, he has already been acquitted.

In the end, the court passed judgment on five of the accused men: Pallme Koenig, Mertens, Goltz, Zuehlsdorff and Brueling. They were given the death sentence, destined to be hanged just as they had hung Rosterg.

LIEUTENANT-COLONEL ALEXANDER SCOTLAND

In his letter, Pallme Koenig was writing to a British officer. This was Lieutenant-Colonel Alexander Scotland. He remarked on the letter in his 1957 book *The London Cage*[3], which caused consternation at MI5 and forced its publication to be delayed by many years.

The London Cage gave greater details about the motivations behind Rosterg's murder. In December 1944 an audacious escape attempt was being planned at the Devizes POW camp. This camp was on current 'loan' to the American forces in Britain to train up their intelligence officers. Despite this, dozens of prisoners joined the 'escape committee' and two prisoners were sent out to survey weak spots in the camp fencing and the location of camp trucks and lorries. The escape was planned for one day during Christmas week, when camp sentries would be fewer due to the leave rota and when Britain would be preoccupied with the festivities.

On the day, key men would be sent out to the car park to commandeer lorries, drive them to the arms store and gather guns. A second group would hurry to the food store to secure rations to be loaded onto the lorries. Several specially selected men were to act as guides to the escape party. They would wait near the lorries until everyone was ready to move with maps of the carefully arranged escape route. The committee accepted that some of these men might be shot and killed in the process.

From the camp they were to head north to Sheffield, where a co-ordinated second escape was being planned. The two escape parties would join forces and form an armed column that would fight its way across the country, heading east to the coast. In the meantime, a radio station would be captured and a message would be signalled to the distant fleet of German warships in Bremen that the prisoners needed transport. The plan was outlandish and had very limited chances of success. But it spooked the War Office enough that all camp sentries across the country found their Christmas leave cancelled.

The detection of the escape plan began with a careless word about the arms stores spoken by a prisoner near a German-speaking American intelligence officer. This led to a full-scale search and investigation, resulting in the discovery that the prisoners had managed to hoard an impressive array of hand weapons. Thirty men were eventually singled out as being involved in the plot and were sent to the London Cage, where Scotland, among others, was able to learn the entire extent of the escape plan. They also quickly realised that the prisoners suspected two of their number as having given away the details of the plot. The first was the ringleader, who admitted the entire affair to the British. Four German prisoners were allowed to question him at the Cage and attacked him in their fury, beating him considerably until the British officers stopped them. This was just one of many dubious instances that were to give the London Cage and Colonel Scotland a very bad reputation.

The second suspect was the liberal-minded, anti-Nazi Wolfgang Rosterg. Scotland stated that Rosterg stirred up trouble at the camp at Comrie by criticising German movements in the Ardennes. Whatever the case, his murder was to result in several men returning to the Cage now under the more serious charges of murder.

Colonel Scotland was not technically involved with internal crimes as he was part of the POW interrogation system. However, he became concerned when it came to the defence of five of the accused men. These five had asked a fellow prisoner to defend them, probably the man named Skrupke in Bienek's note, over the British lawyer who had been assigned to them. Scotland was asked to intercede and managed to persuade the five that British defence lawyers would be the better option.

Colonel Scotland's intercession and generosity in this case, to ensure British justice was obtained fairly, appears to have been a rare instance. His name and his involvement at the London Cage have raised a great deal of controversy. Even in his book, where he consistently denies that Germans were brutalised or tortured at the Cage, there is a sense in his words that he cared little for these men in his charge. Indeed, when he speaks of the ringleader who admitted the Devizes escape plan to the British and his subsequent assault by his colleagues, he calls the thrashing 'well-deserved'.

Scotland was accused of using Gestapo methods on the prisoners to gain intelligence: he refused to give the Red Cross access to the Cage and even detailed in the earlier draft of his book instances of breaches of the Geneva Convention. This information was eventually removed from the book prior to publication. Germans who had been held in London alleged being beaten, pushed down stairs, starved, deprived of sleep and forced to stand to attention for twenty-six hours straight.

In 1943 a formal complaint about abuses at the Cage was sent to the Secretary of State for War by a German who had been held there. Later, at a trial of eighteen Nazis accused of slaughtering fifty escaped Allied prisoners, the defendants listed more complaints of abuse, including the use of electric shock torture. The arch-culprit of these mindless abuses was named as Colonel Scotland.

It is certainly a sordid piece of British history and, compared to much of the sophisticated intelligence-gathering performed at the time, it is a sad reminder that it only takes a few men to return to the brutal methods of interrogation. There is so much evidence from British and German sources that it seems likely that at least some of the complaints were based on truth, and as such it leaves a nasty taint on the British POW system, specifically on the London Cage and the methods of some of its members.

NOTES

1 Death of German POW at Camp 17, Sheffield. The National Archives, Kew. WO 208/4634.

2 Death of German POW at Camp 21, Comrie, Scotland. The National Archives, Kew. WO 208/4633.

3 Lieutenant-Colonel A.P. Scotland (OBE), *The London Cage*, Evans Brothers Limited, 1957.

five

YOU CAN WORK IF YOU WANT

FINDING EMPLOYMENT

Britain was severely short of men as the harvest of 1943 came around. In previous years the army had been brought in to help gather the crops from the fields, but this was no longer possible. The shortage of manpower was a difficult problem. It was partly solved by employing women in the Women's Land Army, but there was still a need for more labour. It was then that the government started to consider the many war prisoners they were holding. Most were fit and able-bodied and doing little in the camps all day. They were a labour force waiting to be employed.

The first prisoners to be offered the chance of work were the Italians. Prisoners volunteered for employment and were paid the same rate as a British worker. Many saw it as an opportunity to escape the claustrophobic camps for a while, as well as a way to alleviate the boredom that came from the monotonous routine of camp life.

Italian volunteers were given greater privileges than those who chose not to work. While they were still technically POWs, they were called co-operators. Prisoners who did not volunteer were termed non-co-operators. Co-operators were sent to labour camps where the barbed-wire fence was partially dismantled and the camp gate often left open.

They were issued with chocolate-brown battledress and shoulder flashes that read 'Italy'. Italian badges of rank could also be worn. The prisoners were issued with 'good conduct' badges after six months of trouble-free working. These badges consisted of an inverted chevron worn on the left sleeve and up to three could be issued, but they could also be forfeited as part of a disciplinary punishment.

Not everyone was reconciled to having the enemy work their fields; some farmers were reluctant to accept the Italians or the Land girls as viable employees. Stories went about of thieving and laziness. The Italians were said to always be complaining or slacking off from their work and the Land girls complained of sexual harassment. But despite these reservations, the farmers and other employers of POWs really had no choice in the matter. Prisoners of war were the only viable workforce available to them.

Italians were employed in a huge range of roles, from agricultural labourers to working on the railways, loading and unloading milk, or cleaning carriages; from working at gas works or the Royal Navy victualling yards to labouring at the coal wharves or factories, or even repairing bomb-damaged properties. The amount of time they worked was in keeping with British civilian or military working hours and they were allowed one rest day a week, usually Sundays.

They could also be employed within the camps, taking over work from the British, such as cooking in the mess, acting as batmen to officers and even taking on clerical work. They received pay equivalent to that given to British workers, but only cooks received the 'skilled' pay rate.

Employing prisoners within the camps freed up men for other work; it was vital for the economy that any manpower available should be exploited. It has been estimated that by employing Italians within the camps, 300 British men could be freed for other work.

There were difficulties, however, that arose from the prisoners. Firstly the men who volunteered refused to work outside their own units after 7 p.m., as this was liable to incur the jealousy of those who had not volunteered and they feared reprisals or being considered traitors.

Secondly, if they worked as batmen, they objected to assisting more than two officers, pointing out that they were only volunteers. It was also felt prudent among the British camp staff to have a contingency plan should the Italians refuse to work and the camp commandant retained a British batman.

Wages were issued as 'token money', notes specially printed for the camps so they could not be used outside. They were redeemable in the camp canteen. Payment rates varied but were increased over time.

By 1945 approximately 3,376 Italians were working in the Metropolitan Police District alone. They were accommodated in camps, hostels or even empty houses.

Until 1944 the Italians wore their chocolate-brown battledress when working, then the Home Office decided to change their uniform and issued them with battledress dyed 'spruce green' and khaki. They had always worn a shoulder flash stating 'Italy', but in addition they now wore a service stripe bearing the Italian national colours.

It was also in 1944 that they began to be allowed greater privileges, which included being able to change part of their weekly wages into sterling for use in local shops. They were allowed to visit the Post Office, where they could send off two airmail letters a month to Allied-occupied Italy, they could use public telephones and watch a film at the cinema. However, pubs and public transport remained off-limits.

Around the prison camps a 5-mile radius existed known as the 'Free Area' (prior to 1944 the radius had only been 2 miles). Italians could wander within this radius as they chose and those allowed bicycles could use them there. There were some limitations though, including the rule that all prisoners were to be back at the camp by 10 p.m. every night.

Originally Italians had only been allowed to speak with British civilians when it was necessary to do so, due to their work duties or within the camp premises. Eventually this was completely relaxed so they were allowed to speak with any member of the public and could accept invitations to private houses. All these new regulations came into operation after 19 August 1944.

However, it was also in 1944 that concerns began to grow about the use of Italians in the local labour force. Aside from the usual complaints of incompetence and poor performance, a new outcry erupted when 1,000 Italian POWs chose to go on strike during harvest time. Needless to say the farmers were furious. The offenders were immediately put in confinement, yet criticism continued that the Italians did not work but wandered around villages laying snares for game.

The War Office had to reiterate that, as the Italians were now co-belligerents and not technically the enemy, POWs who had agreed to aid the war effort were entitled to greater freedoms and liberties than a typical war prisoner. This did little to staunch the flood of outrage. Lord Somerleyton told a meeting of the Suffolk County Agricultural Committee: 'The matter is a scandal in our district. Can't [the Committee] stop the food of those who don't work? No work, no food – that is reasonable. They are having it all their own way.'[1]

There were even calls for the Italians to be removed.

Bring on the Germans

When Italians began to be repatriated, the labour force started to deplete again. The Home Office decided the solution was to enlist the help of German POWs. The number of German POWs in Britain was rapidly rising and it seemed logical that some of these men might be considered as a workforce. Camp commandants were asked to submit lists of suitable prisoners – those without Nazi leanings and who were reliable and trustworthy – and the first 4,000 men were quickly organised to begin work.

The terms of their employment were similar to the Italians, though they had less freedom and initially they were to only work in agriculture and forestry. Sixteen thousand Germans were selected to work in gangs of twelve or more and to occupy recently vacated Italian labour camps.

It had also been arranged that the German POWs would be employed by the United States army forces within the UK, primarily on salvage work. The police were to liaise with the Americans over employment arrangements.

Employing Germans came with its own problems: not all the prisoners were convinced they should be helping the British in any way. At one of the earliest work camps at Braintree, German prisoners had barely arrived before several tried to escape; at Colchester three prisoners succeeded in fleeing the camp.

Yet things did rapidly settle down and the men began to work. One, named Hans Reckel, recorded what had gone on in those first few days:

Work groups were formed, each with one sergeant-major, two unteroffiziere and 27 men. In open lorries, sitting on the tail-boards, we travelled to work in the mornings. On the way we met comrades from the American camp, who were transported in large buses. After a long journey through Braintree and Witham, we stopped on the edge of a large potato field. A foreman was already waiting for us, everyone received the usual wire basket, and then the great potato-picking began.

We were completely out of training and the work was mostly not easy, but we were basically happy to be able to prove our strength away from all the barbed wire, even if accompanied by armed guards. Although our backs got increasingly sore, we worked competitively; everyone wanted to do better than the next man. We drove each other on with words of encouragement.

At the beginning of midday break we were allowed to take two buckets of potatoes to our resting place and cook them for ourselves over the tea stove.

And in the evening we received permission to fill the empty food boxes with windfalls from a nearby orchard, so that we returned to the camp tired and knocked out beyond doubt, but fairly content. Content, too, was a gentleman from London who came to the field on instructions from his ministry and acknowledged that we were 'very good workers'. Later everyone heard it said that we worked 60% better than our predecessors the Italians.[2]

Driving Italy

Italian POWs were allowed to drive transport vehicles themselves. Drivers were selected by the camp commandant and were issued with special papers that stated they had permission to drive. Lorries carried the prisoners from their camp to their work site every day and it was these that the selected Italians drove. Selection of a trustworthy man was essential as the lorries were not given military escorts. The Italians were expected to drive themselves along recognised routes to their place of employment and keep track of the petrol they used on a daily basis.

Italians were also allowed to drive tractors on public highways where it was necessary for the tractor to be moved between fields or farms. The only stipulation to their driving was to demonstrate to the Home Office that they could operate a tractor correctly. It was not even necessary for them to obtain a driving licence.

Italians might also have bicycles; these would usually be provided by an employer, such as a farmer, for the POW to use to cycle back and forth to work. There were, understandably, conditions relating to the use of bicycles. They could only be provided to prisoners who had been previously selected by the military commandant to use them and the farmer was expected to purchase them.

POWs could only use the cycles to travel to and from work and were restricted to a distance of 7 miles from their camp or hostel. If the farm was further away then different transport had to be arranged. Farmers had to take a degree of responsibility for the men they provided the bikes to. If a man using a bicycle did not arrive at his place of employment within half an hour of his expected time, then the farmer had to get in touch with the camp by telephone, using somebody else's if they did not own one.

They were also expected to take care of the bikes and ensure they were safely and securely stored while the Italians were working. Preventing theft of the cycles fell firmly on the employer's shoulders.

In the latter days of the war German POWs also had access to vehicles. This was via the YMCA, who were interested in organising visits to various camps for welfare work during the winter of 1947. Only a small number of Germans, less than six, would be selected for the work. They obviously had to be trustworthy, but also needed to prove that they were capable of driving the vehicles they would be using. To avoid any security risks the POWs would not be issued with civilian driving licences, but instead would be given special authorisation papers under the control of the YMCA.

The Italian POW Police

'The War Office has given discretion to Commands to organise Italian Police Patrols to patrol the exercise area in the vicinity of camps during "off-duty" hours', a typed notice from 28 May 1945 explained.

The Italians were no longer the enemy, they were now co-operators, and as such were allowed greater freedoms. But this in itself could cause problems and the British police forces were overstretched as it was. Organising Italian police patrols eased the problem with the Italians given the responsibility of apprehending any fellow POWs who were behaving improperly or abusing the privileges they had been allowed.

The patrols were to be issued with yellow brassards bearing green 'P's as identification of their new role.

Living In

It was eventually agreed that in certain cases a limited number of prisoners would be allowed to 'live in' on farms where they were employed. Obviously the men chosen for this were reliable and trustworthy and the farmer was fully responsible for their maintenance and behaviour. The prisoner was to live either with the farmer or one of his employees, or in a farm building that was suitable; this could be a barn or outhouse. Though that sounds slightly primitive, farmers were expected to provide prisoners within these buildings with bedding (straw palliasses), artificial lighting, heating, crockery and facilities for washing and a bath. Once the living quarters were agreed upon they were not supposed to be changed without the camp commandant's permission.

Prisoners were to be provided with three meals a day which were expected to be the same as those provided for an ordinary labourer. For this purpose the commandant issued ration books to the POW and the farmer was also allowed to claim the agricultural labourers' extra cheese ration for his guest.

POW wages were in line with the national average – they were to be paid the same as a British worker in the same role. However, payment of wages was never to be made directly from the farmer to the prisoner in his employ and a living allowance of 21*s* had to be deducted from the amount the farmer was to pay.

The farmer was completely responsible for his charge and had to ensure that the prisoner did not leave his farm on weekdays except where certain arrangements had been made for him to visit a religious service or special occasion. On Sundays prisoners were allowed to leave the farm but were not to enter local villages, shops or houses other than the farmer's, and they were not supposed to talk to the general public, though on many occasions these rules were bent and the farmer turned a blind eye.

Prisoners were not supposed to attend a Roman Catholic Mass alone; the farmer or someone he had nominated was to escort them. Nor were prisoners allowed to go outside or remain outside during the blackout, though exceptions were made under certain conditions, such as when a prisoner had the duty of milking the farm cows and had to be working before daylight.

The military were careful to state that POWs were not to send letters other than those they were allowed to send through the camp system, nor were they to be given money or gifts by the British public and, logically, they were not to be allowed the use of firearms.

How stringently these rules were kept to would depend on the farmer. While it was stated that the prisoners would remain under the observation of the camps and regular visits would be made to the farms, how often this actually happened is debatable. Farmers and their families often became companionable with the prisoners and stopped viewing them as an enemy captive and considered them a friend. One farmer even left his farm to the POW who had worked for him.

Money Matters

Working outside the camps gave the prisoner the advantage of earning a wage that he could spend. While money was earned in sterling it was given to the POW in the form of credits to be spent on the camp premises. By 1947 a prisoner could earn 6*s* a week which he could draw to use on purchases in the NAAFI, along with twelve bonus cigarettes. In addition, he could earn a 9s weekly bonus for good work. He could not touch this bonus amount, however, as it was to be kept and paid to him in marks on his return to Germany. Over the course of a year this meant a prisoner could earn £15 12s in regular wages and £23 8s as a bonus. The prisoner would spend the majority of his regular pay in Britain, but his bonus was in effect his savings for his return home.

Yet the bonus money was paid at a rate of 15 marks to the British pound, whereas the current official exchange rate in Germany was 40 marks to the pound. The POW had to spend this money in Germany and, as the purchasing rate within the German black market was 230 marks to the pound, the men realised that for all their hard work they had really only earned around 30s for the entire year's bonus when the exchange rate was taken into account.

Understandably the men were cynical and disinterested in this bonus. So they saw no benefit in doing anything more than the minimum amount of work required from them. Farmers employing the POWs and desiring higher quality work found it necessary to offer them illegal incentives in the form of their own money, cigarettes, beer and clothes. Since the farmers were already paying £4 to the Ministry of Agriculture for having a prisoner labour force on their land, adding illegal inducements to the bill was hardly satisfactory. Neither prisoner nor farmer was getting a fair deal.

It was suggested by the chief constable at Huntingdon that to improve the situation prisoners should be paid £1 a week, be allowed to spend some of this within Britain and be able to send the rest to Germany, if they desired, at a fair exchange rate.

He also felt that if prisoners were able to spend their money more freely this would reduce many of the instances of theft the police had noted, which were mainly of small items such as eggs, wood, fruit, potatoes and leather. These crimes had been particularly rife during the previous winter when the prisoners had little work to keep them occupied due to severe weather. The chief constable also argued that if it was made clear that a man discovered to be guilty of these petty crimes would lose his opportunity to earn and spend money, this would prevent much of the thieving.

He hoped that the authorities might consider allowing certain German prisoners who had volunteered from the labour forces to live in complete freedom outside the camps, perhaps just reporting to the police on a monthly basis. Thus they could earn and spend their money just like a regular workman. He felt the result of this relaxation would be an improvement in the men's work. He also had other suggestions, including commenting about men volunteering to stay and work in Britain rather than being immediately repatriated, and the effect this might have on the men they were working with who were still prisoners.

How much attention was paid to the chief constable's suggestions is questionable. As the regulations governing POWs were under review anyway, by the time he wrote his letter many of his points had already been discussed and new proposals arranged. He was told bluntly that allowing the men to live in complete freedom outside the camps would require a 'fundamental change in their status'. They could no longer be considered prisoners of war, but would be enemy alien civilians and would no longer be under military control. The government was not prepared to give up this control unless it could be proved to be absolutely necessary. Therefore, the idea of German prisoners becoming civilians was quickly quashed.

Saving Up

Another advantage of earning a wage was that prisoners were able to save money for when they returned home. While this was a mostly informal process, in one or two camps Italian prisoners invested money in the British National Savings Scheme and received their own stamp cards. The amount they invested varied between 6d and a few pounds.

The investments seemed harmless enough but when the matter came to the attention of the War Office they saw things differently: 'It has now been decided, for very good reasons, that enemy prisoners of war shall not be allowed to invest money in this manner and the task of redeeming the money now arises.'[3]

The War Office's sudden intervention caused some alarm, especially as it seemed the Treasury was not entirely in agreement with it. In a handwritten letter dated 20 February 1942, it was stated:

> that the Treasury was not satisfied with the reason furnished by the War Office. It is that if the Italian prisoners were allowed to invest their pay in savings the Germans might find this an excuse to confiscate the pay of prisoners of war in their hands and whilst the German Government might quite possibly repudiate its liabilities at the end of the war the British Government certainly does not intend to do so.

The argument had returned to the matter of reprisals; even a seemingly harmless situation as allowing Italian prisoners to join the National Savings Scheme could, in the eyes of the War Office, lead to British POWs suffering. How justified they were in this idea is hard to know. Only a few Italians ever participated in the scheme and it is not even clear if the Germans ever knew anything about it.

But the matter was settled. The War Office forwarded the Italians' savings stamp books to the Post Office savings bank. A total of 189 books had been collected and the combined amount the Italians had saved was £152 18s 6d – a considerable sum that would now be redeemed to them.

With the books came a detailed list of the amounts each prisoner had saved, ranging from 2s to over £6. Three of the biggest savers were Calisto Brachino, who managed to save £5 5s, Vincenzo Clerico, who saved £5 9s, and Aniello Gargano, who saved £6 11s.

Scuffles, Assault and Fraud

In the late 1940s stories frequently popped up in newspapers involving prisoners of war. In some cases they were the instigators of trouble, in others they were the victims. It is hardly surprising that they should appear in the news when so many were working in Britain and freely mingling with the local population.

Two German POWs, Rudolf Peters and Hans Siggelkow, were accused of assaulting a police officer in Cromer late one morning in December 1948. Police Constable Fleming had discovered the men sitting in a shelter at 7.20 a.m. on a Sunday morning. They had no passes but told him they had come from Matlask and had missed the last bus the previous night. Fleming arrested them.

At the police station the men became difficult; they began speaking in German to each other and insisting to Fleming that they wanted to be allowed to leave and return to Matlask. When this did not happen Peters kicked Fleming in the stomach, there was a brief struggle and then the two prisoners fled the station. A short time later, at 8.40 a.m., they were spotted again by Fleming and two constables in a police car and re-arrested.

In court Siggelkow acted as interpreter for Peters. They talked briefly in German and then Siggelkow replied to the court in English: 'All right, we did it.' They received one month's imprisonment.

In another case British law was on the side of a German POW who had been misled and robbed by a local man. Friedrich Haumann had been working at Holveston Hall when he met a man named 'Steve'. Steve told him that his sister worked in a cigarette shop and could get him a packet of cigarettes for 3s instead of the usual 3s 4d. Friedrich liked the sound of that and gave Steve a £1 note, but the cigarettes never materialised, nor did Friedrich get his money back.

Steve was eventually identified as Stephen Denton, who was known for obtaining money under false pretences; he had previously told a local man, Mr Craske, that he was in the wood trade and could get him cheap timber. Craske had paid him 10s for a load of wood that never appeared. Foolishly, at an earlier date, Craske had also agreed to buy eight rose trees off Mr Denton at the cost of 2s 6d each. Unsurprisingly, these trees also failed to appear.

Denton was sentenced to six months for obtaining money fraudulently from Friedrich, but only received three months for fooling Mr Craske, despite the sum being larger in that case.

WHEN TROUBLE BREWS

POW labour was not always popular among the British populace for a number of reasons, the simplest often being that the prisoners appeared to be taking work away from the local men. In fact, the government had made it clear that no POW could perform work where there was a British workforce that could supply it. However, in some instances the local men were not as skilled at certain tasks as the prisoners and delays in the progress of work could occur if the prisoners were removed in favour of British workers. The government saw no logic in doing this, yet that did not dissipate the negative feelings among some of the native population.

In May 1945 trouble was brewing at Bethnal Green, London. Italian POWs had been sent to a hostel in Sceptre Road by the Ministry of Works; from there they went daily to work on different projects for the Ministry of War Transport and other departments. Feelings were running high among the locals and there had been several incidents between civilians and Italians, seeming to focus around the hostel. The police felt the problem could easily escalate and wanted the men moved, but those involved with the administration of the work teams were less convinced. They took the view that moving the prisoners could affect the progress of work they were currently attending to.

The military were also far from convinced that the men needed to be moved. In their view the incidents between civilians and Italians had been 'minor' and they considered it the police's responsibility to maintain civil order.

All the problems had occurred earlier in the year, the first happening on 20 February. A local man, Mr Frank Newmeir of Portland Place, made a complaint against two Italian privates, Campione and Calistroni. Newmeir claimed that around 7 p.m. that night his daughter Lilian, aged 16, had returned home from work and complained to her father that two Italians had been following her and whistling at her.

Mr Newmeir went outside with his daughter and she pointed out two Italian soldiers standing at the corner of the road. Newmeir marched over to the men and told them: 'Leave the girls alone when they come home from work.' He then stated that Campione had struck him in the face and taken up a fighting stance, while Calistroni said something in Italian which Newmeir didn't understand but suspected it was to urge on Campione.

Newmeir then struck Campione in the face and the two Italians ran off. The police were unable to take statements from the POWs as neither spoke English, but they did observe that Mr Newmeir had three small cuts on his face and Campione had a slight swelling over his left eye.

The next incident happened around 7.10 p.m. on 18 March. Three local youths, Ernest Seaman, aged 16, Thomas Charles Davies, aged 18, and Arthur Perry, aged 15, all claimed that while crossing waste ground near Sceptre Road an Italian assaulted them, striking out at them with his fist. When they tried to defend themselves they alleged the Italian drew a knife and chased them a short distance before returning to his camp.

The police made enquiries but could shed little light on the matter. No one at the Italian camp could provide any useful information and the police decided to take no further action.

The next incident happened on 24 March between 2.30 p.m. and 3.15 p.m. Two Italians, Andrea Candela and Tommaso Carvisigno, were walking along the road at the same time as Charles Fountain. Fountain explained that he had bumped into the men and they had turned on him, while the Italians stated that Fountain had called them 'F— Italian bastards!' Both sides agreed a scuffle had ensued and several blows were struck. Carvisigno confessed to kicking a civilian on the backside, while Fountain was adamant that he had been knocked to the floor and repeatedly kicked.

Candela and Carvisigno then tried to return to their camp but Fountain and another man followed them. Carvisigno said that the smaller of the two men following them was carrying an axe and that he turned and grappled with this man, whereupon the axe was dropped. Carvisigno threw the man and at this point he says he noticed a knife on the ground. He picked up the knife, intending to take it back to the camp, but a crowd had gathered and were pursuing him, so out of fear he threw away the knife.

Candela confirmed his companion's story and said that he had picked the axe up off the ground after it was dropped with the intention of taking it back to camp. He went a different route to Carvisigno but, when he was nearly at Sceptre Road, he was caught by his pursuers who wrenched the axe off him and, Candela declared, threw it and struck him in the back as he fled.

There were four witnesses to the scuffle but none could give a clear or full picture of what had happened and it seemed that the axe and knife were never actually used during the brawl. For his part Fountain said he just wanted to forget about the whole incident and the matter was dropped.

Other occurrences were more mundane but could still cause consternation. On the afternoon of 8 April a special constable patrolling near the Sceptre Road camp spotted an Italian handing a parcel to a young girl. The girl was Doreen Watson, aged 13, who refused to tell the police what was in the parcel and was taken to the police station. There the parcel was found to contain a small rug, a piano cover and four dressing-table covers. The police were instantly suspicious as to how an Italian POW happened to have these items in his possession. They were concerned that the items were stolen property, possibly from bomb-damaged houses he had been working on. Doreen told the police that her mother had given her a letter to deliver to an Italian named 'Tony', and told her that she would receive a parcel. Doreen also delivered a letter from another woman that she only knew by her first name, Lily.

The police went to the camp and identified 'Tony' as Antonio Ciurlia. Through an interpreter Antonio said that he had brought the items with him from Africa and that he had not received any letter delivered by Doreen. Unable to find any letter in his possession, the police had to return to investigating the British women instead.

Doreen's mother was Mrs Lilian Wilson, Doreen being illegitimate. She said that while the Italians were working on bomb-damaged houses in her neighbourhood she had met Tony and become friendly with him. When his work was finished she promised to write to him at the Sceptre Road camp, but she denied any knowledge of the items he had given Doreen or that she was expecting to receive a parcel from him.

Lily was Mrs Lily Ellen Franklin; her letter was addressed to a different Italian named 'Tony' who she also met while he was working on bomb-damaged buildings and became friendly with. Shortly afterwards she received a letter from him asking to meet her, but she did not keep the appointment and wrote a reply which was the letter Doreen had handed over.

However, Doreen's report of the events was rather damning to both women. She explained that both her mother and Lily had become quite friendly with the men while they were working in the neighbourhood and that her mother had even visited the Italians' camp to see Tony. On 8 April both her mother and Lily gave Doreen letters to deliver to the men. Mrs Wilson told her daughter that she might be given a rug in exchange. Doreen went to the camp and waited outside the railings until the two Tonys appeared. She handed over the letters and they gave her a rug and 'some blue things'. She then went to buy an ice cream but was stopped by the police. Fearing that the rug and other items the Italians had given her had been taken from the debris of ruined houses, she tried to run away but was caught and had to give a statement.

The police continued to make enquiries about the property Antonio had handed to Doreen, but there was no evidence to contradict his story that he had brought it from Africa, so eventually they returned everything to him.

While the incident was relatively minor, both Franklin and Wilson, who had become friendly with the Italian men, were married women. Situations such as this were liable to arouse tensions among jealous husbands, or even those living locally who thought it unsuitable for a British woman to consort with an Italian.

MORE TROUBLE

The Italians seem to have found themselves always caught up in trouble while working in London. Usually the incidents were fairly minor, such as when police found two Italians drinking in a pub. The men were asked to leave and did so without any trouble. Sometimes disputes resulted in a scuffle. Police regularly took reports on fights between the Italian POWs and British civilians.

On 23 December 1944 a Mr Harold Skinner reported to the police that he had been attacked by two Italians who had descended from a coal lorry at Fulham and assaulted him with their fists. He said he had fallen and struck his head against iron railings. The Italians admitted to the assault but insisted they had been provoked and the police were happy to leave the matter in the hands of the camp commandant and no further action was taken.

A nastier incident involved Italian sergeant Guiseppi Giannoccaro, who was in charge of a working party at New Cross railway station. He had become friendly towards a female carriage cleaner also working at the station and was spoken to by the woman's foreman. Giannoccaro attacked the man, biting his ear and neck. Subsequently he was given a court martial and sentenced to two years' imprisonment.

The most common complaint was of Italians molesting women and girls in the area. On the whole the complaints were unfounded – often the 'molested' girl was in fact a willing party. When a report was made that Italians were accosting nurses at the Clare Hall hospital in South Mimms the police investigated but found no evidence, aside from the matron witnessing Italians congregating in the lane beside the hospital with the seeming intention of making contact with the nurses. She assured them that she had heard no rumours of her female staff associating with the Italians but did agree to put the lane 'out of bounds'. Another complaint by the father of a Land Army girl, who claimed his daughter had been insulted by an Italian, was equally found to be without basis. However, in some cases the complaint was upheld and was dealt with by the camp commandant in liaison with the police.

The police could rarely find evidence that the Italians were breaching any camp rules to be with women. They were also aware that in many cases the local women sought out the Italians either at their camps or while they were working and attempted to make conversation with them. The police instigated patrols at certain hotspots, including camps at South Harrow and Osterly Park, to prevent British women from approaching the men.

Nevertheless, the press got hold of the story and reported in the papers about the behaviour of the Italian POWs. The media attention was so prominent that the Home Office felt it necessary to ask for reports to be submitted on the behaviour and conduct of the prisoners. These reports made it clear that the press was blowing the problem out of all proportion.

The main difficulty was that complaints could be malicious and driven by resentment. Where work, or lack of it, was not the cause of local animosity, it could be housing arrangements. In certain areas Italians were accommodated in private houses that were empty. Locals resented this when their own properties were bombed and they found themselves homeless; they believed the Italians were living in houses that should have been given to them. Eventually the authorities removed POWs from private dwellings and the anger towards them swiftly dissipated.

Other problems surrounded the perceived special treatment the prisoners got. British workers who had to queue up for public transport envied the special transport the Italians received to deliver them to their places of employment. But, interestingly, there were no concerns about Italians being able to visit the local shops or cinema.

Dangerous Work – Bomb Disposal

The Geneva Convention clearly stated that prisoners of war could not undertake any work that was directly linked to the war effort, including the manufacture of munitions or the transporting of equipment to Allied soldiers. It also stipulated that prisoners could not undertake war work that was hazardous. Despite this, and despite Britain's normally scrupulous adherence to the Convention's stipulations, in 1948 some German prisoners were set to work in bomb disposal.

Prior to the Germans' employment, the British authorities had attempted to have Italian POWs working in munitions factories after Italy had agreed to peace with the Allies. On that occasion the Geneva Convention had tied their hands, and despite being promised that regulations would change, enabling them to transfer Italians to the factories, this never occurred and munitions production was hampered.

To get around this fact with the Germans the War Office released 260 POWs to civilian status, initially for agricultural work, but then bomb disposal in London. Another seventy-five were released from Fairmile camp in Surrey. As early as 1945 Germans were performing work which might include lifting mines, detecting unexploded missiles and the general handling of munitions.

The situation was complex. After 1948 a number of Germans chose to remain in Britain and work here; they were no longer classified as POWs but did not quite qualify for civilian status and remained under the close watch of both the military and the police. The men had previously been employed while living in the prisoner camps. Now that officially all POWs had been repatriated, Britain was still in need of extra workers. The workforce that had come from the Italian and German prisoners had suddenly evaporated and there was a void of labour. Arrangements were made that those Germans who desired to remain working in the UK could.

But the government could not simply turn over these men to their own devices; the war was not long past and trust for the Germans had yet to be truly developed. The workers who chose to remain were sent on leave to Germany between December 1948 and January 1949, and upon their return the men had to report to the police immediately. They could not perform any work other than that which they had been engaged in just prior to going on leave. If they wanted to go into a different business or profession they could not do so without the Secretary of State's permission, and the men were only to be in Britain temporarily and would leave on the date specified by the Secretary of State.

There were those men who, for a variety of reasons, did not wish to return to Germany, even on leave. For these men discharge forms were organised which effectively enabled them to stay in the UK indefinitely. The forms were relatively basic, just asking for details such as name, address, occupation, date and place of birth, and details of any family, in particular any children who were minors. The form was in English and German and had to be signed by the holder. It was intended that by 31 December 1948 all former POWs would be discharged in this way.

Eventually employment restrictions were relaxed. A press release was issued stating that any prisoner who had lived in the UK under civilian status for four years could apply to have the restrictions lifted and to work in whatever industry they chose. The prisoners mainly concerned were Italians, Ukrainians and Germans. The Italians had had civilian status since late 1943 when Italy became a 'co-belligerent', so they were entitled to apply in 1948. The Germans could not apply until 1951 at the earliest and some had to wait until 1952.

While the Italians could not work in bomb disposal, they were employed in other areas where work could sometimes be 'disagreeable'. On the railways Italians were paid a 'dirty work' allowance at a similar rate to British workers for jobs that were unpleasant. This included tunnel work, the 'clearing of drains of an exceptionally dirty character' and the handling of raw materials at docks, such as bulk sulphur, oily tubes, cement, loose salted hides, dextrine, floating timber, Canadian white flour, lime, dates in oil, ore in bulk, manure in bags, barytes, coal and coke, and, perhaps the most disagreeable job to us today, raw asbestos.

Cooking His Way to England

Employment was a major concern for POWs returning to Germany – many would find themselves without work or doing jobs that were far beneath their usual skills. Unsurprising then, that any opportunity for paid work was gladly accepted, even if it meant moving to England.

Such was Karl Westermayer's case. He was due to be repatriated to the British zone in Germany but was currently working as a cook for Major-General H.E. Pyman in the Middle East. The major-general had asked Westermayer if he would like to remain in his employ and become his cook in England. Westermayer accepted on the condition that his wife and family might come with him.

The major-general, however, had given little thought to the red tape his employment offer would involve. On 24 March 1948 Captain Willcocks, PA to the chief of staff, wrote to the British headquarters in Berlin to discover what would need to be done to bring Westermayer and his family to Britain. The records tail off as to what became of Westermayer and his job offer, but he was not the only POW who had so impressed his captor that he was asked to continue working in Britain.

Notes

1 R. Douglas Brown, *East Anglia 1944*, Hyperion, 1990.
2 Ibid.
3 Treasury decision against allowing investment in National Savings Stamps by Italian POWs, 1942. The National Archives, Kew. NSC 21/286.

six

A GIRL'S GOTTA DO WHAT A GIRL'S GOTTA DO ...

FRATERNISATION

During the early part of the war civilian association with prisoners was strictly forbidden. People breaking these restrictions could face fines, and several court actions are recorded where civilians, in particular women, were caught meeting and talking with POWs and ended up before a judge.

Such was the case of a 34-year-old woman from Barrow who, in May 1943, found herself before the Bury St Edmunds courts for 'fraternising with an Italian prisoner of war, thereby committing an act likely to prejudice discipline'.[1] The mother of three was fined £1, the prosecuting solicitor saying she was in the habit of talking to one particular POW in a quiet place in the late evening. In her defence the woman said she would not have got to know the Italian had she not been working on a farm with several prisoners. She also stated that many women talked with the men and would carry on doing so.

In another case at Great Bardfield an act of kindness by two Land girls landed them in court. They had been ditching on the same farm as several Italian prisoners. When the Italians complained about being lonely the girls agreed to write to them. These letters were intercepted but the authorities did concede that the correspondence was purely personal and contained nothing to harm national security or anything immoral. During the case a police witness was asked if he was aware of people fraternising with the Italians, to which he said he was but that they were 'trying to stamp it out'.

At Huntingdon three girls were charged with sending letters to Italians other than 'by post'. Once again there was no implication of immorality in the communications, but the prosecuting solicitor was still shocked, saying: 'The national enemy is the private enemy, and these men with whom there were these intimate friendships are men whose purpose it has been to destroy everything these women enjoyed, and to kill our own flesh and blood.'

Of the three girls, two had written the letters and one, though British, had Italian parents and so could speak fluently with the prisoners. They were each fined £1. One of the girls was the daughter of the landlord of the local pub and had delivered the letters via an Italian who visited the pub daily.

It could seem almost petty that the courts would fine people for such obvious acts of kindness. At Braintree a Belgian soldier, his wife and a ward nurse were all in trouble for being involved in sending a care package to three sick Italian POWs. The Belgian soldier had been a patient at the hospital at the same time as the prisoners and during his two-month stay he presumably became quite friendly with the Italians. When he left the hospital he asked his wife to send a package of food and cigarettes to the prisoners who were still hospitalised. This she did, addressing the package to the hospital and asking the ward nurse to deliver it.

All three were brought to court on the matter and pleaded ignorance of the regulations and that they had only acted out of kindness. The prosecuting solicitor agreed that this seemed to be the case and the action was dismissed, though they had to pay costs.

With more working parties being organised outside the camps, it became necessary to clarify the restrictions on the prisoners. They were not to speak with British civilians other than when it was necessary for them to do so to perform their work. This regulation was particularly strict when it came to prisoners associating with women or girls. It clearly stated: 'Any instance in which it is shown that a prisoner of war has disregarded this order and in particular has entertained or attempted advances of a sexual nature will render him liable to rigorous and exemplary action.' This is one of the few documents that makes clear mention of sexual relationships between local women and POWs – a problem that was no doubt rife and could cause endless friction between the local community and the prisoners.

There were other limitations the prisoners had to adhere to. They could not accept food, money or cigarettes from members of the public, nor any article which could be seen to assist them in an escape attempt. They could not enter public houses, places of amusement or shops other than in the course of their duty and could not use public transport.

The rules on fraternisation were not lifted until 1946 but many broke the regulations, considering them arbitrary and unkind. In Caernarvonshire a commotion was caused when the police posted notices around the area warning locals about associating with POWs working in the locality. Apparently the locals resented the posters, perhaps considering them an insult on their own common sense and law-abiding natures. The situation started to become tricky when it was realised that the posters were in fact stirring up sympathy for the POWs. A letter was even sent to the Secretary of State asking him to organise the removal of the posters.

The chief constable in Caernarvon had other views on the matter. He had not heard of any complaints about the posters, though upon making enquiries did discover a certain amount of resentment towards them. He had, nevertheless, received complaints about POWs: firstly that one prisoner had been going to farms asking for and collecting eggs; secondly that a POW was alleged to be regularly working and not wearing his prisoner uniform; and thirdly that on VE-day a German prisoner-of-war football team played against a local team at Pencaenewydd after sharing a meal supplied by the local celebrations committee in the chapel vestry. Considering these clear infringements, the chief constable considered the posters absolutely necessary to remind locals of the regulations and rules.

Whatever the authorities said there was still a lot of sympathy for the Italian and German prisoners. The Italians in particular seemed keen to 'fit in'. Some made a significant impact on the British population. In April 1943 young surgeon Lieutenant Mario Luchi, a member of the Royal Italian Navy, received acclaim from locals when he risked his life to save a 6-year-old British boy from drowning in the River Cam. Luchi had formally been a swimmer for Padua University and used his skills to save the child. The public were so impressed and grateful to him that they called for him to be immediately repatriated if he wanted to go. The authorities were less keen on this suggestion but did award Luchi a Royal Humane Society parchment, presented to him by the Mayor of Cambridge.

THE FAIR, THE BRAWL AND THE MISSING MARINE

I don't see it is any good complaining that the place is unsuitable for a POW camp, after all, no local residents exactly welcome having such a camp in their locality. A staff of 23 to cope with 2,300 prisoners seems somewhat inadequate, but I suppose there is nothing we can do about it.[2]

So read a letter from the Metropolitan Police at Great Scotland Yard about camp 144 near Kew Green, London, where there had been some recent problems. The camp housed Italian prisoners, and since the Italian surrender in late 1943, when they became co-belligerents, the Italian POWs in Britain had been allowed increased freedoms. They were not technically enemy prisoners anymore but they were not citizens either.

The Italians enjoyed their new freedom, leaving the camp regularly and visiting local fairs and pubs and associating with girls and women. This fraternisation did not sit well with some of the locals and by 1945 tensions were rising to breaking point.

At 9.32 p.m. on 28 June 1945 the police were informed that trouble had erupted between Italian POWs and local youths near Kew Bridge, Kew Green. The trouble had begun, it seemed, when an Italian POW had approached a British woman. Two police constables were immediately sent out and by 10 p.m. they were reporting that the disturbance was subsiding. However, an Italian and a British soldier had both been stabbed during the fight. The former had been sent to the camp to await transport to the hospital, while the latter had been taken to Brentford Cottage hospital in an American Jeep.

The injured Italian was 39-year-old Private Giuseppe Giunti, who had been stabbed in the left breast. The resident Italian military doctor did not consider the wound serious but felt the injured man was not in a fit condition to be interviewed. Giuseppe was eventually removed by military ambulance to Kingston County hospital.

Meanwhile, the injured British soldier, Private Leslie Friday, had been transferred to the Staines emergency hospital suffering from four stab wounds in his back. His wounds were also not considered serious and he was able to make a short statement to the police.

Friday stated that he had been in the Boathouse pub with his brother when a row began outside between Italians and British civilians. When the row turned into a fight, Friday and another soldier went outside to intervene. As he approached the group an Italian grabbed his arm and he felt several sharp blows to his back. Friday did not immediately realise he had been stabbed but when he saw that the Italian was carrying a penknife he knew what had injured him. He was still in the POW's grasp and the man managed to stab him in the hand.

Feeling blood running down his back, Friday shouted out that the Italian had a knife and finally the POW released his grip on the private's arm. Unfortunately, Friday informed the police that he did not think he could recognise the Italian again.

The police then interviewed Italian witnesses. One, Corporal Pietro Liparotti, gave a detailed account of what he had seen. He had walked to the Boathouse with Private Giunti. When they reached the pub, they went down some steps near it and walked along the riverside for 200 yards. As they turned back and headed for the stairs they noticed two British sailors, several soldiers and civilians standing there. They estimated them to be all aged between 18 and 20. Liparotti was approached by a sailor who asked him: 'Any women down this road?'

Liparotti answered in broken English: 'I see no women in this road.'

A sailor then began to pull up his sleeves and say to the Italians: 'Come on then, fight.'

Liparotti quickly answered again in his stuttering English: 'I not fight. I no give trouble you, you not give trouble me.'

The sailor then swore at them and told them to 'get away'. Liparotti told the police he was only too eager to comply and headed for the steps with Giunti. A civilian then approached them and repeated: 'Come on, fight.'

Once again Liparotti tried to avoid trouble, answering: 'Me no fight, me go Camp.'

At this point, Liparotti stated, the crowd formed two circles, one around Giunti and one around himself. He saw Giunti being forced towards the public house where men went inside and returned with bottles and glasses which they smashed. Liparotti managed to escape the crowd and ran up the stairs where he saw four more Italians approaching. He shouted: 'Go away, there are a lot of people here.'

Liparotti then saw a sailor draw a knife from the top of his trousers. Giunti had somehow also extracted himself from the crowd and together with him and the other Italians, Liparotti ran to the top of the stairs that led to the bridge and attempted to escape. By now a considerable crowd had gathered and were throwing all 'kind of things' at the Italians. The British sailor was still brandishing the knife and several of the POWs had to avoid his blows.

Once again Liparotti and the four Italians managed to get away, but when he looked back he saw Giunti being held by a man who was threatening him with his fist and saying, 'Go to Camp'. Liparotti tried to release his friend from the man's grip but could not, so he grabbed a stick and struck the man across the back of the neck. Giunti was finally freed but the man Liparotti had struck told him that he was wounded. The Italians ran away and met up with three more who Liparotti asked to escort Giunti back to the camp, which they did.

Liparotti also provided a description of the sailor who had brandished the knife. He was young, about 5ft 3in or 5ft 4in tall, well built and wearing a British sailor's uniform. His hair was light chestnut and he had a round face with pale complexion and was clean-shaven. Liparotti said he would recognise him again if he saw him.

The police, however, could not find a person matching the description and were apparently not convinced by the entire honesty of Liparotti's statement; in the report it was noted: 'It is peculiar that although Liparotti was protecting himself from the Britishers who were around him he was able to note a fair detail what happened to Giunti.'

They interviewed several other Italians who were involved in the fight. They all said they saw British soldiers with knives, broken glass and pieces of wood. Each of these witnesses had received some slight wound and one stated that he saw a sailor draw a new type of bayonet, but didn't see anyone actually stabbed with it. Some even suggested that the British were in possession of firearms, but the police dismissed this allegation as none of their main witnesses had made mention of such an important detail.

The man who Liparotti said had been holding Giunti and threatening him with his fist was identified by the police as Mr George Harold Long of Maze Road, Kew. Mr Long was walking along the bridge at about 9.15 p.m. when he spotted a group of Italians being chased by several British soldiers and sailors along the riverside. He intervened and attempted to break up the fight, telling the Italians to return to their camp. The British servicemen abandoned the chase and the Italians hastened away. But when Mr Long got to the top of the steps from the riverside he saw about a dozen Italians who had armed themselves with broken bottles and glasses and sticks.

One of them struck at him, losing their cap in the process. Mr Long warded off the blow and snatched up the cap before heading off to the POW camp, where he made a complaint to a British officer.

Mr Long concluded by saying he witnessed Italians throw glasses, bottles and sticks at the British troops, but did not see anything thrown back by the British. He saw no one brandishing a knife or bayonet, witnessed no one being stabbed and emphasised that he had not thrown any blows.

The Italian witnesses had also mentioned that a woman had started shouting at the crowd from a nearby house. The police identified her as Mrs Annie Louisa Bavin, who lived at Kew Green and had heard noises outside her bedroom window. When she looked out she saw five local youths and a British sailor fighting with a solitary Italian.

Mrs Bavin made it clear that the Italian was not defending himself and she shouted out the window: 'Here, stop that, I'll phone the police.'

She moved away from the window but shortly returned and heard a youth tell his friends: 'Look out, she's coming back, the cops are coming.' One of the youths then turned to Mrs Bavin and told her: 'You side with the Italians.'

Mrs Bavin's response was: 'Not at all, but it is not fair for all of you to be on to him.'

The youth retorted: 'That Italian has been talking to my sister.'

The youths then ran off to the nearby tennis courts and Mrs Bavin saw nothing else, though she did feel she could recognise the youth that had accosted her.

On 2 July the police finally spoke with the injured Giunti. His story was almost identical to Liparotti's, but he did add that during the fight his hat fell off and, straightening up after retrieving it, he saw a sailor coming towards him with a short bayonet. He described the blade as flat, about 10in long, and it was this weapon that stabbed him in the left breast. He was doubtful, though, that he could recognise the sailor again and the only other thing he remembered was being helped back to the camp by two Italians. He did not see anyone else with a knife or bayonet.

The police then went on to interview four British witnesses, Baker, Angel, Wells and Taylor, each a member of a local gang of youths who were responsible for a great deal of trouble around the Kew Bridge area. Their stories were not given much credence, especially as it was clear they had rehearsed them among each other to ensure their statements matched.

They first interviewed John Edward Baker aged 14½, who was sitting with his friends on the bridge when he saw a young woman standing at the side of the pub. She was approached by an Italian and he estimated there were 'about six or eight other Italians standing nearby'.

Baker felt that the girl did not welcome the Italian's attentions and he then saw a British sailor approach the girl who, it seemed to him, she had been waiting for. The sailor exchanged words with the Italian and then hit him. The other Italians came forward and Baker and his pals ran down the steps to the riverside to watch the fight and saw the sailor joined by three soldiers.

Baker declared that most of the Italians had drawn knives, 'the ordinary type of penknife'. It appeared to Baker and his friends that the British were getting the worst of the fight so they decided to join in. Baker picked up a stick and claimed that during the brawl an Italian with a knife attacked him, cutting his palm. He struck the man with his stick across the head, whereupon the POW fled. All the Italians were then chased up the steps to the bridge and Baker stated that both sides were throwing things at each other. The fight only ceased with the police's arrival.

Baker repeated that many of the Italians were brandishing knives and that he saw one British soldier with a short black bayonet, but he never saw him use it and doubted he would recognise the man again.

Richard William Angel, aged 15½, told a very similar story to Baker, adding that when one Italian drew a knife they formed a circle around him and he tried to stab them, but only succeeded in causing minor wounds to Baker and another lad called Turner. Angel provided a description of the Italian: 'dressed in a green battle dress and light green pullover with a high neck.'

Angel said he witnessed the Italian stab a British soldier in the back and hand, at which point a British sailor ran over and kicked the attacker between the legs. The Italian fell down and then ran off. Everyone descended into a general fight and several people, including Angel, went into the pub and got bottles and glasses to use as weapons.

Once again the police were uncertain of their witness' credibility:

I should point out here that Angel is the only person who says he saw the Italian stab the British soldier. He says he was with his friends who had formed a circle around the Italian and it should follow that if Angel is telling the truth his friends should also have seen the incident. They describe an Italian who they saw fighting with the British soldier who was later found to be stabbed. This description of course fits with the one seen by Angel but against this the injured soldier, Private Friday, is very definite when he says that the Italian who stabbed him was wearing a brown battle dress.

Angel was also one of several youths arrested the night after the fight for using insulting words and behaviour.

William Frederick Wells, aged 14, could only confirm that he saw a sailor kick the Italian between the legs and that the POWs were carrying knives. Eric Frederick Charles Taylor, aged 18½, could only provide details of the fight, saw no one stabbed, but had received a cut to his left wrist. The lads also stated that there were thirty to forty Italians against twenty British, which added little to the accuracy of their statements.

The police went on to interview Frank Friday, Private Leslie Friday's brother, an able seaman on leave at Richmond. He had been dancing in the Boathouse when someone said there was a fight going on outside. Frank looked about for his brother and when he could not see him he went outside. As he approached the crowd an Italian hit him across the face and forehead with a stick. Friday joined in the brawl and shortly after spotted his brother. Leslie's hand was bleeding and he also noticed there was blood on his shirt. Leslie saw his brother and said: 'Don't worry, Frank, he has only gashed my hand.'

Frank then pointed out the blood on his brother's shirt and Leslie added: 'I did not know anything was done to my back.'

Frank Friday then lost his temper and started beating an Italian with his fists until an ATS girl and a civilian dragged him away. He stopped a Jeep being driven by an American and asked him if he would take his injured brother to the hospital. Both brothers drove off with the American to the Brentford Cottage hospital. Frank Friday stated that he could not recognise anyone involved in the fight and saw no one actually stab anyone. He was not carrying a knife as he never did when on leave.

The police went back to interview the injured Leslie Friday again. He had given a short statement on the night of the attack, but the next day when the police spoke to him he claimed not to feel well enough to talk to them and they arranged a meeting for 1 July. The police officer in charge was unconvinced by the excuse and suspected Leslie wanted to discuss his story with his brother Frank before saying anymore.

Leslie Friday repeated to the police that he had been in the Boathouse when the fight began and had gone out with a lot of other people and saw an Italian hitting a civilian with a stick. He ran over to intervene but four or five more Italians appeared and a general fight broke out.

Friday grappled with an Italian who put his arm around him and thumped him in the back with, as Leslie then believed, his fist. He then punched him in the hand and Friday felt a sharp pain. He realised he was bleeding and shouted out that the Italian had a knife and his attacker ran off. Otherwise his story corresponded with Frank's.

Leslie Friday was adamant the Italian was wearing dark brown, which contradicted Richard Angel's story. The police felt that it would be impossible for the dark-brown Italian battledress to be mistakenly identified as green and so dismissed Angel's testimony on the matter.

The police conclusion was that there were no reliable witnesses who could identify any specific person as the one who stabbed Friday. The police found Angel to be too unreliable to consider letting him view an identity parade of Italians just so he could 'pick out some person he thinks may be the culprit'.

The majority of British witness statements testified that the Italians outnumbered the British by nearly double. Except for one significant statement. That of British Private Sidney George Etheridge, who the police saw as a 'perfectly disinterested party'. He said that he saw no one carrying a knife and that the British outnumbered the Italians.

The biggest problem the police faced was that the Boathouse was a popular pub for soldiers and sailors on leave. Therefore, most of the clientele were not 'regulars' but casual customers, making it harder for any clear identifications to be made. The Boathouse also seems to have been a frequent trouble spot. Prior to the arrival of Italians in the district, fights had often broken out between American solders and British servicemen there.

The Italians were known in the area for associating with local women and the police felt that this was the real catalyst behind the fight. The British officer in charge of camp 144 often received letters from local girls addressed to one of the POWs; he even occasionally received letters addressed to him asking him not to punish the Italians when they were caught by the civil police fraternising with local women.

The matter was far from settled, however. On Sunday 1 July the police received news that trouble had once more erupted between Italians and the British at the Boathouse. Heading down there, they found that the Italians had already returned to their camp, but a few moments later a group of 100–200 of the POWs returned, armed with sticks.

The sight of a large number of uniformed police officers turned them away, but only for 100 yards or so before they became problematic and the police had to draw their truncheons. Eventually the group was quietened and the Italians returned peacefully to their camp. The catalyst for this fight seemed to stem from British sailors and local youths letting off fireworks near the Italians, which the POWs presumed were pistol shots.

The police felt that several aspects led to Kew Green becoming a prime spot for conflict. Firstly, the Italians had limited recreation provisions for exercise at their camp and so were allowed to leave the grounds after finishing work. Secondly, people that the police termed 'of the rough element' would travel from Brentford and Chiswick to Kew and if they spotted any Italian speaking with a British woman they would cause trouble.

As the matter could not be satisfactorily resolved and no one could be prosecuted for the stabbing of Giunti or Friday, the police arrived at a compromise with the British camp officer. The Boathouse was placed 'out of bounds' and police were given the authority to search any POW that they suspected of carrying a weapon.

The solution was far from ideal, so when trouble erupted on August Bank Holiday 1945 at the local fair on Kew Green, many were not surprised:

> It is unfortunate that these Italian Co-operators were allowed to visit this fair on August Bank Holiday. It should have been realised by the camp authorities that with holiday crowds about, repatriated soldiers and the likelihood of a few people in a slightly drunken and quarrelsome state, brawls would be inevitable.
>
> We are fortunate that this fracas did not develop into something far more serious. Only one person was hurt, an Italian Co-operator who was detained in hospital.

The chief constable explained shortly after the event: the incident occurred at 3.15 p.m. and Arcangelo Conte was the Italian who was injured. He was taken to the Royal hospital in Richmond with a cut upper lip and was detained under observation for shock. Though he could not speak English, Arcangelo explained to the police what had happened through the camp interpreter. He stated: 'A solider came up to my brother and I and said he had been a prisoner in Germany. I said to my brother "This man is drunk" and walked away. We returned a little later and someone hit me. I don't know who.'

The police inspector in charge of the case visited the scene of the assault and then interviewed several British soldiers who were witnesses to the affray. They all told the same story; that an unidentified Italian struck a woman for no apparent reason. An English marine, who could not be traced or identified, intervened and the result was a free fight in which soldiers, civilians and prisoners all became involved. The police could find no evidence to implicate Arcangelo as the cause of the fight or that he had actually taken part in the brawl, nor could they find the woman who was supposedly assaulted.

The police found it impossible to identify the real cause or instigators of the disturbance: 'The truth of this matter cannot be ascertained but I have no doubt at all that this man was attacked by some person inflamed with drink but who may have seen this Italian associating with a female. It does not seem likely that we shall trace the offender.'

The immediate reaction to the fight was for the camp commandant to put the fair out of bounds to the Italians and forbid them from congregating in groups any larger than three. Kew Green, which had previously been the Italians' unofficial meeting spot, was also placed out of bounds and the prisoners took to travelling further afield, which seemed to alleviate some of the local tensions.

The Italians were viewed as lascivious by certain members of the local population. Irate complaints filtered in to the police, listing vague suggestions of the moral crimes the Italians were committing. An anonymous author penned the following in October 1945:

> It is not safe for any decent woman to be on the highway after dark for fear of molestation in some form or other from these men.
>
> For instance, yesterday evening a lady, whilst proceeding from Kew Gardens Railway Station to Maze Road, was accosted by eight of these Italians who attempted to get into conversation with her. You must agree that this is a terrifying experience. Further more I have information that this kind of behaviour is indulged in by these men throughout the immediate neighbourhood. In many cases their general conduct is both beastly and degrading to the extreme.[3]

Due to the writer failing to name themselves, the police felt there was little they could do to discover if the allegations were true or false. The camp commandant, on the other hand, felt it his responsibility to reply to the woman while also asking the police to keep him informed about any location where Italians were known to congregate. He explained to the anonymous informant that he was unaware of any complaints against the men in his charge but if she would care to contact him he would 'give her every assistance to identify the offenders and [in] any case afford her every possible protection'.

There was a sense that the authorities felt the complaint to be spiteful and unfounded – certainly the anonymity of the author did little to make the accusation credible.

Another letter, written on 3 May 1946, from the Joint Committee of all Ratepayers' Associations of Richmond addressed to the police superintendent, sums up certain local attitudes to their European guests:

> on April 30th last; many complaints were brought to our notice of the disgusting behaviour of the Italian prisoners of war. After much discussion, I was requested to write to your good self protesting in the strongest possible terms and to enquire what was being done to control these uninvited and extremely ill-behaved men?
>
> It is realised that owing to the smaller force at your disposal it is impossible for your men to be everywhere but in view of the nature of the

complaints – molestation of women and girls – the Committee sincerely trust that some further and stricter steps will be enforced in the future.

The district commander's response to the ratepayers' complaint was short and to the point:

> I rather feel that this present letter of complaint from 'Joint Committee of all Ratepayers' Associations of Richmond' is somewhat exaggerated.
>
> Police are alive to the situation and we do everything with the limited manpower at our disposal to deal with the situation.

Possibly the police's view of the exaggeration of the ratepayers' complaints was due to the fact that many of the local women and those further afield chose to travel to Kew Green and visit the prisoners. Police patrols had already dealt with sixteen girls under the age of 16 who had been fraternising with the Italians.

Even so, an inspector was sent to the camp to investigate the matter. He spoke with the Italian 'Officer of the Day', who informed him that the problem was caused by some new Italian prisoners who had recently been sent to the camp. They were described as having poor discipline and requiring greater supervision than the other men. The officer added: 'knowing no women, they [the new prisoners] had set about striking up acquaintance very brazenly and, in his opinion, that was probably the cause of this complaint.'[4]

Not entirely satisfied with the explanation, the inspector spoke with the camp adjutant, Captain Allen, who advised him that he intended to post extra military patrols around Kew from midday on Saturday and Sunday, which seemed to have the desired effect of improving the Italians' behaviour.

The camp commandant had also had words with the men, threatening them with the removal of their co-operator status or even their repatriation rights if they were reported against again. And while the threats were mostly empty, the men were convinced enough to try and avoid getting into any future trouble.

Mr Russell-Evans, the author of the 'Ratepayers' Association' letter, was also met with and informed of the measures being taken. Possibly feeling guilty that his comments had caused such commotion, Mr Russell-Evans began to retract his complaint, explaining that it 'did not really concern fraternisation; it was the way in which the Italians openly made advances to and even jostled women that was people's concern'.

Feeling there was a certain amount of bluster in Mr Russell-Evans' initial letter, the inspector pressed him on the matter:

> the statement in the letter that 'many complaints' were received by the 'Ratepayer's Association' surprised me. I now learn from the writer of the letter that no actual complaints were received, but when the question of these prisoners being housed in Kew area was discussed, members of the Association at the meeting brought forward complaints. I am quite satisfied that to say women and girls are molested is a gross exaggeration of the situation. Some prisoners do smile at women when they receive encouragement and there is no doubt that women do 'run after' these prisoners.

In summing up his report on the matter, the inspector stated:

> It is felt that the position regarding fraternisation is best left as it is, unless some other aggravating aspect enters into it. There are between twelve and fifteen hundred of these prisoners, and girls, who are more than willing parties, come from all parts of London to meet and associate with them ...
>
> Hitherto, there has been the impression that any action taken against these prisoners would not produce much result, as confinement to barracks means they get out of work, and they do not object to this for periods. However, the Commandant says the means he has at his disposal are most effective ...
>
> It is probable that the severe warning that the prisoners have been given will produce good results, and will be the best means of bringing about improvement.

A comment written in black ink at the bottom of the reports concludes:

> I do not think there is molestation of our women by these Italians, but if encouraged – as they are by some – they endeavour to build up an acquaintance. On the 11th of May an Italian Corporal was found embracing a woman from Ilford at Richmond Towpath. She was a willing party; the Corporal has been reported.

Fortunately, the situation was due to resolve itself. The camp was disbanding and all the prisoners were due to leave and be repatriated by 20 September 1946. They had been at Kew for a total of nineteen months.

It was anticipated that a working party of 2,000 Germans would eventually take up residence at the camp, but only twenty arrived and finally it was agreed that the camp would be left to the GPO, who were already occupying some of the buildings. Watchmen were employed to ensure the camp did not become home to squatters and the Kew Green affair, probably much to the relief of the police, came to an end.

MARRIED MEN

Once the rules on fraternisation had been lifted, understandably relationships began to form between those POWs who were working outside the camps and local women. Indeed, furtive relationships had begun before the restrictions were lifted, but now they no longer needed to be clandestine.

Not everyone agreed with British women consorting with the enemy and some found themselves criticised or insulted for their choice, though few were deterred.

The government recognised that these new relationships could cause problems legally. Within British law, if a woman was to marry a German she would give up her British nationality and no provisions could be made for her to be able to live with her new husband as he would remain in the prison camp. He would not be allowed extra privileges that other POWs could not have and there were no provisions in place for keeping the husband in Britain after repatriation began. However, as long as both parties were aware of these conditions and happy to abide by them, then no obstacle would be put in the way of them marrying.

But the repatriation problem was untenable for the newly married couples. In April 1948 a notice was issued by the Secretary of State declaring his decision that any German who had married a woman of 'British stock' could now apply to be released from prisoner-of-war status and that all such applications would be dealt with sympathetically. The news was good for those men who had married British women, particularly as the applications would purely be judged on his marital status and not on any future employment prospects. Once released from his status as a POW, a man could be employed in any line of work or set up his own business if he chose. As the notice explained, he would be 'as free as a British subject'.

To obtain his release the POW had to take his marriage certificate and his wife's birth certificate to his camp commandant, who would then pass the information to the War Office and subsequently the Home Office for a decision.

The process was not completely straightforward, however, as the notice stated that applications would be refused where evidence from the camp commandant or from the police suggested that the particular POW 'would not be a desirable addition to the foreign population of this country'.

If a prisoner's application was successful he would receive a formal letter from his camp commandant that he would then take to a police station so he could be registered under the Aliens' Order and receive his Aliens' Registration Certificate. He was then entitled to register for his national ID card, ration books and clothing coupons.

However, the notice did not extend to men who were only engaged to a British woman. In these cases repatriation could be delayed for the man in question to give him and his fiancée time to arrange their wedding. He could then apply to be released from POW status as soon as the church bells stopped ringing.

FOOTBALL AND FAIR PLAY

Football was a major part of camp life and most had suitable football pitches on site for the men to practise on. Understandably, many became quite proficient and regular Saturday afternoon matches were held within the camps.

In 1947 the LCC started to press for the Ministry of Works to relinquish land it was using within the London parks. The ministry was housing POW working parties in hutted compounds and were not eager to give up the land, even after the prisoners were repatriated, stating that it might be necessary to provide accommodation for civilian Poles coming to take over the work.

The LCC was not impressed; it pointed out that the prisoners' camp quarters included space for a football pitch. Could they not relinquish that at least and send the men to play at the public pitches?

The military authorities debated the matter. One camp commandant raised the issue that friction might arise between the general public and the prisoners if they had to compete for time on the pitches. But the LCC was not to be deterred. The Metropolitan Police were questioned and it was agreed that as long as the prisoners did not use the pitches on Saturdays, Sundays or early closing days, and that local clubs were given priority booking, there should be no real problem.

But they did concede that this did not apply to the camp at Wormwood Scrubs, as the local sports field was already a sore spot among the community due to the local football club regularly using it. Therefore, adding prisoners' matches to the already strained situation might not be the best move.

Lieutenant-Colonel Collins at the Ministry of Works had other ideas. In a letter dated 27 June he reiterated the conditions on which prisoners should be allowed to use public pitches and then replied: 'I am afraid the scheme cannot go under these conditions and we shall have to call the whole thing off.'

He set forth his argument that if the plan was to go ahead it would mean that the only times the prisoners could play on the public pitches would be during their working hours and as such they would never get a chance to play. And if they were to see the public using their pitches, as the LCC wanted, yet could not use the other pitches available to them, resentment would quickly develop. Collins concluded that such a situation would raise complaints on the prisoners' behalf both by the public and with the Houses of Parliament.

The letter had a certain note of satisfaction to it as Collins probably felt he had won the case. Yet more damage to the LCC's request was done at a meeting held in August when various reasons were given for why the camp pitches could not be released for public use. These included that recreation space was a requirement for POW sites and that, while prisoners were now allowed greater freedom, due to complaints from the public it was seen as wise to encourage them to spend their free time (especially the younger prisoners) within the camp confines. Demand for the pitches within the LCC parks was simply too great and it was not seen as feasible to ask the public to share the pitches on equal terms with the POWs. Finally, when the LCC suggested that the public might be allowed to use the camp pitches when the prisoners were not there, such as when they were working, the objection was raised that in doing so it meant the public could also enter the huts, and this was not tenable.

Eventually, concession was made that once the prisoners had been repatriated and the civilian workers moved in there would no longer be a requirement to retain the camp pitches and they would be handed back to the LCC.

THE PRISONER-OF-WAR ASSISTANCE SOCIETY

There were those whose apparent interest in helping POWs in Britain was far from charitable or without ulterior motives. Such became the case of the Prisoner-of-War Assistance Society (POWAS). Operating between 1945 and 1948, their initial remit seemed innocent enough. The POWAS workers originally 'were content to do all they could in a friendly spirit for any POW who came within reach of their service'.[5]

The founder members of the organisation were Mrs Violet Foss and her daughter Mary. They began their campaign in 1945 with letters published in the correspondence column of the *Catholic Herald*, where they asked that POWs should be treated more leniently and that repatriation should be speedy.

Via correspondence in the *Catholic Herald*, the founder members drew together people who were interested in the welfare of war prisoners and formed them into the society. But they also drew the attention of the Metropolitan Police's special branch. Violet Foss was a former detainee, strongly pro-Nazi and once a member of the Imperial Fascist League run by Mr Arnold Leese. She was known to have maintained contacts with a number of fascists within Britain. Nevertheless, the early aims of the society appeared genuine enough and many people driven by purely humanitarian concerns gave their support to POWAS.

At regular times the society petitioned the government for speedier repatriation, permission for a parcel service for the men and greater freedoms for prisoners. All of which were eventually granted, though whether this was due to POWAS or coincidence is debatable.

By 1946 the society was under police scrutiny again when it became apparent they were unofficially and illegally gathering large supplies of cigarettes, woolies, comforts, food and sweets and were distributing these to prisoners they had made contact with.

Soon the society expanded its role to include seeking out missing members of a POW's family and receiving parcels from prisoners' relatives in America or elsewhere and passing them on, until eventually they were able to send parcels direct.

With restrictions lifting in regards to prisoners sending parcels to Germany, Italy and Austria, the society became an unofficial postal service for the men, even issuing their own postage labels which would ensure the parcels arrived safely. In addition, the society ran an 'adoption' scheme, where British families 'adopted' a German family and began corresponding with them.

Gifts were given to camps comprising books, devotional materials, musical instruments, chocolate and cigarettes. Difficult or personal issues were often negotiated between the prisoners, their families and the authorities by the society, and they also had a hand in helping men gain compassionate repatriation after the war.

The intentions of the society seemed honest; even their letterhead stated they were non-political and non-partisan, but this was far from the truth.

Letters between society members, though discreet, began to hint at the true motives of the project's leaders. In one written to Mrs Leese of Guildford, Surrey, there was talk of keeping out the 'wrong sort' from the society and of helping 'the real victims of the war'. The letter continued by talking about a man only referred to as R.H., a high-ranking member of the Nazi party, who appears to have been facing trial. He was connected to some of the members of the society and had apparently informed the letter writer that trial verdicts were becoming milder and he anticipated being released by 21 May. The writer was only prepared to reveal certain facts and R.H. would uncover more when they could meet in person, though he was interested in carrying on 'Friendship' contacts and developing an organisation along those lines.

In another letter to Mrs and Mr Leese, written by Mrs Foss, she talks about the German repatriation and how their 'scheme' has many advocates in different countries. The Red Cross and even the War Office were sending cases to POWAS for them to deal with which were usually relationship problems the prisoners might be facing upon their return home. Mrs Foss remarked, 'we at least have the assurance that the right people get our help and our service is kept for them'. Who these 'right people' were was to become clearer in future correspondence.

Mary Foss, Mrs Foss' daughter, meanwhile, was busy taking any opportunity she could to contact POWs or enter camps. During August 1946 a Lieutenant Victor Watts from the Alton POW camp was in town when he noticed a box of twenty cigarettes lying on the floor with a card attached to them. Upon picking them up he was approached by a woman who identified herself as Mary Foss, a member of POWAS. She asked the lieutenant if it was possible for her to come into the camp as the society had a great deal of money which it wished to spend on sending parcels to prisoners.

Watts told her she would need to speak to the War Office and left the matter at that. Later he discovered the society was not recognised by the War Office.

On 8 November 1946 a German POW named Heinz Schilde escaped from his camp; on 10 November he returned to the camp and surrendered himself. Despite the weather being bad, Schilde was dry and clean-shaven – clearly he had been housed somewhere during his time from the camp. On being questioned Schilde said he had been hiding in a wood. When asked if he had been staying with Mary Foss he declined to answer but later admitted that he had seen Miss Foss during the previous three months, though he refused to say that it was she who had housed him. In his possession was a letter from Germany which made reference to Mary.

Mrs Foss was under financial pressures. She was unwell and surviving on her old-age pension and the income her daughter brought in from a small job. This did not, however, deter her from her voluntary work with POWAS, though some of the bitterness about her situation was creeping through in her letters and revealing her true motives: 'having been ROBBED by the "Chosen" of everything almost that we possessed, I am now down to the old-age pension.'

The Metropolitan Police's special branch had taken an interest in the society's dealings and was making notes about its leaders. Mrs Foss was known to be a fascist and honorary treasurer of POWAS and she had written in 1947 to another member of the society, Mrs Sharland, also a well-known fascist, asking her to post a letter to a German woman named Frau Helga Prollius. In the letter to Mrs Sharland, Mrs Foss stated: 'it [the letter to Frau Prollius] is to a woman who has forgotten her noble heritage or is unworthy of it. I don't want her mixed up with this address.'

Apparently Frau Prollius had recently made laudatory comments about conditions in England during an interview with the *Daily Herald* and Mrs Foss, in her letter, instructs her to remember the advantages and benefits Hitler had brought to Germany. Her letter was blunt and nasty:

Frau Prollius, Madam. If you are a German woman note this: in view of your interview in Daily Herald & your statements made on a few hours knowledge of England: was there ever a country where family life was so encouraged as Germany under your late Führer? In contrast take a look at our divorce courts and life in London! If you are an elderly woman or even a plain one, try to get a seat on a bus in the rush hour if you want to see our marvellous courtesy. Take a look at our poor women if you think so much of our smartness & is such smartness such a wonderful asset to the nation? As to some of our hens being named after politicians: the average English person respects their hens too much and politicians too little for this to be a rule. Also remember Hitler's bird sanctuary & his laws protecting animals &

cease using your imagination because there are many loyal English homes where that Führer, whom you probably 'Heiled' when it suited you, <u>is respected</u> as one who could have saved your country from its present plight & Europe from its future one. One thing you <u>can</u> with confidence know about us. We have no real respect for people who 'Heiled' yesterday and mock or criticise today those who at least gave Germany prosperity rather than chaos. You would do more good building up your broken country even as he did after [illegible], than you will do paying empty compliments to the 'Liberators'.

The police also reported that Mrs Foss had been paid a visit by a Miss M. Hill, a lady of 80 who had come from Bath to meet her. Mrs Foss later said about her:

[Miss Hill] has stood all through the war in defence of Hitler and his ideals. She now wishes to make a trust fund for us to help <u>certain</u> German families. She came all the way from Bath to see us, the frailest thing I have ever seen looking about 100 and just tottering but so brilliant and active in her mind – so thrilled to meet the boys and tell her ideals and so sorry she was not with us in Holloway … She has never belonged to any society or political party – just thought things out for herself and stood up publicly and told people what she thought through the war. Then she heard of us and it was her first contact.

Mrs Foss also wrote about a Mr Frederick Lohr, who the police knew as an anarchist and regular speaker at Hyde Park. She said that he had just returned from Italy and reported that no one speaks their mind on the Continent now, and that anyone who speaks out of turn or is disliked by their neighbours is labelled a fascist and 'can be bumped off (especially in Italy) with no one daring to take any notice'.

It had now become clear to special branch that POWAS was a fascist organisation only concerned with helping prisoners who shared their ideals and beliefs about spreading the fascist cause. They were making inroads into Europe, developing contacts and hoping to send Mary Foss to Germany as a representative of their cause. Mrs Foss herself was becoming less discreet in her comments about her views.

In reference to an article by Commander Stephen King-Hall in which he said, 'Let us beware that the Nazi leaders from their nameless and dishonoured tombs do not claim the final victory', Mrs Foss responded: 'I yet believe it will be written under a certain name what I have written under the picture of its owner, "*Du hast dooh gesiegt!*" [You have definitely won!]'

The Foss family were now all involved in the cause: Mary Foss was engaged to a German POW; Mrs Foss' son Alan was also known to special branch as pro-Nazi; and their friend Mrs Sharland received anti-Semitic material from America as well as closer to home. This included thirty cards sent by Mrs Foss, similar to visiting cards, upon which were written 'Boycott the Jews', which she was instructed to leave in libraries, telephone boxes and waiting rooms. But perhaps aware she was under surveillance by the police, Mrs Sharland disposed of the cards.

Mrs Foss was elated that she was managing to 'aid' so many POWs in Britain but also irritated that other organisations were jumping on the bandwagon, though not in their political leanings. She remarked:

> We worked hard when it was DANGEROUS, UNPOPULAR & ILLEGAL, but of course now that it is safe, 'Everybody's doing it', as the old song says and we are a bit irritated with the societies – some by no means Aryan or English or Christian who have gone all pro-German to save their faces! We are however keeping to our original idea and emphasising it, that we are NOT a RELIEF society to 'Save Europe' but FRIENDS of the peoples which, in the name of our country have been destroyed, or that there has been an attempt to destroy. We want to make reparation and to build up a friendship & we can do this by attending to the individual cases, also we can tell those who help us that what is done, IS done for an individual and not for a 'group' which may contain many who are neither German, Austrian nor in dire need.

Other members of the society were also drawing attention to themselves. Mr George Goldie, vice-chairman of POWAS, had been going into POW camps taking men's home addresses and sending post on their behalf. This contravened regulations and enabled uncensored letters to slip to Germany. The police took Mr Goldie in for questioning and he confessed what he had been doing, but said he had only sent postcards on certain prisoners' behalves to try and ascertain the whereabouts and condition of their families. On being asked about a letter he had sent to America on behalf of a German woman named M. Neuerburg, Goldie explained that she had been a friend before the war and he was only writing to see if he could find out if any of her relatives were in POW camps in America.

After being reminded that it was an offence for a civilian to enter a POW camp or accept items for transport, Goldie assured the police that he would not offend against regulations again.

As the political aims of the association started to become more apparent, and well-known fascists began to give their support, other members became uncomfortable. The society's chairman, Mr M. Huntley, resigned when he heard that Lady Clare Annesley, a known fascist, had joined. He refused to have any connection with her, even by being in the same society.

Huntley was known to the police as a man of unstable temperament who, in 1941, had served a prison sentence for trying to persuade several members of HM Forces to desert. He was known to be an adamant pacifist and Italophile. It appeared he had joined the society to aid Italian POWs still remaining in England, and not because of a generalised concern for the fate of POWs whatever nationality. While initially he seemed to have been unconcerned and even encouraging of POWAS' aims, this started to change as time went on. However, he was not pro-Nazi. He would later become a member of the Friends of Italy Society.

Prior to resigning, Huntley had received a letter from a woman who simply named herself Marianna, who outlined her own concerns for the cause:

> The more I think about it, the more anxious I become that those Hitlerites should not be in our Society. They are up to no good. It worries me, because I feel sure they will get you into trouble in the end. I think it would be dreadful if all your efforts and work and sacrifices should be wasted because of a handful of Fifth Columnists. They are like the Communists who work in the same underhand deceitful way ...
>
> I rejoiced to see your letter in the C.H. [*Catholic Herald*] this week but rather thought they had cut a lot of it out. I noticed they printed Miss Foss's letter in full.

While overtly the society was remaining true to its aims of helping prisoners, the large number of fascist, anti-Semitic pro-Nazis, some politically prominent, that were becoming members was causing growing concern about its real objectives. Additionally, there were unsubstantiated reports that POWAS was being used as a means to disseminate fascist propaganda among the German prisoners.

The society was becoming a victim of its own success. So many requests and offers of help were being sent that Mrs Foss and her daughter, who seem to have been solely in charge of correspondence, found themselves inadequate to cope with the demands. Meanwhile, the society had turned its notice to the famine that was arising in certain parts of post-war Germany. It had received a letter from Germany on the subject, but defended its lack of aid by stating that the British government was committing 'deliberate murder' by not allowing food parcels to be sent from Britain to Germany. POWAS continued its criticism, failing to take into account the political complexities of dealing with the defeated Germany, the ongoing post-war demands and shortages in Britain, and the continual need for caution as there were those still intent on gathering support for World War III, who the Society themselves were aiding. In one letter, excuses for not sending food parcels to starving Germans took on a historical aspect, the writer claiming his reasons extended back to 1919. For a society all too eager to overlook Hitler's crimes in favour of his 'great works', POWAS was incredibly keen to accuse the British government of 'murder'.

POWAS' political motives were highly controversial, but for many POWs all they saw was a welcoming outstretched hand of friendship. With the war over and repatriation slow, the men's morale was dropping. They saw the system of choosing who returned and when as biased, even corrupt. They felt that ardent Nazis were being chosen over themselves even when the British had insisted this would not be the case, simply because those men had better connections. While much of their discontent was inevitable and their complaints based largely on rumour and anger, it would be unfair to say that no German managed to 'queue jump' to get home ahead of others. In these circumstances POWAS could seem a welcome friend.

However, the society was destined to slowly fade away. The police don't seem to have done anything other than watch and listen. As Germany settled down to rebuilding its tattered self and the last prisoners finally returned home, POWAS no longer had a cause. They disappeared as discreetly as they had begun.

NOTES

1 R. Douglas Brown, *East Anglia 1943*, Hyperion Books, 1990.
2 Brawls between Italian POWs and British service men and civilians in Kew Green area 1945–46. The National Archives, Kew. MEPO 2/6492.
3 Ibid.
4 Inspector's report dated 11 May 1946. The National Archives, Kew. MEP 2/6871.
5 The Prisoner of War Assistance Society. The National Archives, Kew. KV 5/64.

seven

AND THEN THERE WAS PEACE

When the war ended, Europe and Britain were in varying states of chaos. Damaged both physically and mentally, dealing with the post-war problems now became the next battle.

There was no longer a Germany. The country had no government after the death of Hitler and this meant no peace treaty could be signed. Instead, Germany was divided into 'zones' with Britain, America, France and Russia all occupying their own portion. Berlin, as the capital, was the only issue; no one nation could be allowed to dominate that city, so it was split between the victors.

Next on the agenda was dealing with the various prisoners being held in Allied countries and the gradual release of British and American POWs. There were millions of prisoners being held across the nations and these men all had to be processed, released and transported home. This was no mean feat and it makes it more understandable why repatriation was not completed until 1948.

There was also the political aspect of post-war Germany – what was it to do now? Rebuild itself? Form a new government? What would happen when the Allies withdrew from the country? Would World War III become inevitable?

Fearful of what the future might hold, the Americans and British embarked on programmes of re-education which taught German men about democracy, free thought and open debate. In the meantime, they were trying to assist those Germans who had been unfortunate enough to be captured by the Soviet Union.

KEEPING AN EYE ON THE RUSSIANS

Approximately 3 million Germans had been captured by the Russians, though not all had survived their imprisonment. As the war ended, the full horrors of the Russian camps started to become apparent.

In September 1946 the Russians made an announcement that they would be sending 20,000 Germans they were holding prisoner back to the British zone, where they had originally resided. The British authorities agreed to receive a 'trial sample' of 1,500 men at Friedland. On arriving the POWs were in a terrible state. The British report reads: 'The condition of POWs received under this exchange has been extremely poor, the majority suffering from malnutrition and many from hunger oedemas.'

Eventually, the full 20,000 would be returned, all ill and starving. The minister for Reconstruction, Labour and Welfare requested a German medical commission to examine 12,260 of the German POWs at the British-run transit camp in Friedland between 4 September and 10 October 1946. The commission was headed by a Dr Schoen, who was head of the medical clinic at the University of Gottingen. He brought three specialists with him, a surgeon, a dermatologist and a hygienist, to examine the men.

Each German was initially examined by a camp physician and then, according to the results, sent to the relevant specialist in Schoen's team. Three barracks were turned over to the specialists' work, another housed the Rontgen-ray (a type of x-ray) machine, while a fifth was turned into a laboratory. Another three barracks served as waiting rooms and a place for the prisoners to be weighed and measured.

The majority of the returning men had been in Russian camps for one and a half to two years; a few had served three years. Their camps had been in regions such as Siberia, Karelija, central Russia, the Volga region, the Ukraine and in Latvia, Poland, Lithuania and the Njemen region. Their living quarters varied from stone buildings, wooden huts and hospitals to tents and dugouts. Most of these places could be heated but the men stated there was rarely enough fuel to do so.

For clothing the men used their own uniforms, old Russian uniforms or working clothes. In winter old padded cotton suits and underwear were handed out. In some camps clothing could be changed every eight to fourteen days, in others every three to ten weeks, while in one dire example every six to eighteen months. The POWs had to wash their own clothes and a main complaint was the lack of soap.

The men considered their food rations insufficient, containing little fat or meat, which was much needed to provide their bodies with the energy to keep warm. In most camps the men received soup three times a day with a daily allowance of bread that varied between 500g and 1,200g. The bread was often damp, which had to be taken into account when assessing its weight. In some camps the prisoners were also given a daily ration of up to 250g of a gruel called *kash*.

Considering the work the men had to do, the food was seriously inadequate. The prisoners were employed in woods, mines, quarries, factories, hospitals, in the construction or reparation of buildings and roads, and on the railways. On average the men worked between eight and twelve hours, though in the forests they often worked from dawn until dusk. Those men who produced more than 110 per cent of the requested amount of labour could have an extra 300g of bread with their ration, but only if they could prove that they had done so.

The list of illnesses and deaths of prisoners related to the British was even more staggering. The men reported that 88 men had passed from diphtheria, 2 from scarlet fever, 115 from typhoid fever, 477 from dysentery, 835 from malaria, 186 from typhus, 30 from hepatitis, 3 from tularemia, 86 from wolhynian fever, 529 from pneumonia, 381 from pleurisy and 197 from nephritis. Added to this, among the survivors 140 men had had limbs amputated for different reasons and 315 were suffering from cullulitis and leg ulcers.

The medical commission classified the majority of the men according to their age and found that 70.36 per cent were aged between 30 and 49, while only 0.25 per cent were between 60 and 69, which equated to twenty-six men. Of the total, 2.51 per cent (295 men) were aged between 17 and 19, which suggests that some of the Germans entered Russian captivity as young as 15.

The prisoners were also assessed for their level of malnutrition by comparing their weight to their height. This could, in some cases, be difficult to calculate as many of the men were suffering from oedema. Oedema is the build-up of fluid in the tissues of the body caused by acute malnutrition. The fluid inflated the weight of the men suffering from the condition, thus giving an inaccurate appearance of more weight than was actually due to fat and muscle. To try and establish a more accurate picture, men with obvious oedema were ruled out from the statistics; but even so, some may have been suffering without visible signs. Taking this into account, among the different age groups 20–21 per cent, on average, were underweight. The worst underweight individual was a prisoner who was 46 per cent underweight – he was 172cm tall but only weighed 39kg. The medical commission had no way of telling whether this man was suffering from invisible oedema, in which case he may have actually been more underweight than what they recorded.

In most cases the specialists were certain that given proper care and nutrition the men would be recovered enough to work normally within six months. Yet in some instances they saw that it would take a longer time than was 'calculable' for the men to regain their fitness. Most men showed signs of vitamin deficiency, the worst deficiency being a lack of vitamin A which 1,542 were suffering from. Nearly all men had lost teeth: 365 had lost three or more.

It was remarked that the men looked much older than their age, and that most had very low blood pressure. Many men complained of shortness of breath, dizziness, vertigo, palpitations and fainting spells, which the specialists put down in part to the lowered blood pressure.

In four cases, the deaths of prisoners could be shown, after postmortem, to be a direct result of starvation. Tuberculosis was rife among the men and in 10 per cent of the number examined, the Rontgen-ray showed this when the chest was x-rayed. The specialists calculated that the occurrence of active tuberculosis (whereby the prisoner was suffering from the condition at the time of being examined) was ten times more frequent than among the normal German civilian population. In some cases it was expected that the prisoner would soon die from the disease.

Tuberculosis wasn't the only respiratory condition the men were suffering from; there were 11 cases of pneumonia, 128 of pleurisy, 312 of chronic bronchitis, and 63 cases of bronchial asthma.

Stomach complaints were also rife among the prisoners; there were 339 cases of chronic gastritis and enteritis caused by the poor quality and inadequate supplies of food. The men's stomachs had reacted to the poor diet in part by shutting down; the specialists noted a lack of hydrochloric acid secretions in the stomach and 'insufficient production of the enzymes of digestion'. Their bodies were struggling to reabsorb food and, combined with infectious gastric diseases, this had made some men severely ill. There were 10 cases of men with a prolapse of the rectum due to general muscle weakness, but surprisingly there were only 50 cases of stomach ulcers. Of the prisoners, 194 were also suffering from kidney or urinary tract disease.

The neurological condition of the men was understandably poor. Of those examined there were 18 cases of epilepsy, 1 case of schizophrenia, 13 cases of what the specialists described as 'abnormal mental reactions' and

22 cases of central and 45 cases of peripheral nerve paralysis – these latter two were probably caused by either diphtheria or a similar disease, or a deficiency of vitamin D.

Eye conditions were fortunately minimal; there were 18 cases of conjunctivitis but none appeared to have left long-term damage. Seventy-two men had lost an eye, but there were only 2 cases of deafness. Skin conditions were quite common, especially among the severely under-nourished. There were 444 cases of scabies, a rate 100 times higher than that expected among a civilian population. Many had been suffering with skin problems for more than six months. The most common infectious disease among the returning prisoners was malaria; more than two-thirds had fallen sick from the illness in 1946. Some showed signs of a hardened spleen and were thought to be suffering from chronic malaria.

The cold conditions of the camp sites had led many to suffer from frostbite. The specialists noted 177 cases of which 34 had developed frostbite while in captivity. Frostbite had led to 117 men losing limbs. Of these, 49 men were considered fit enough to work on their return home, though 30 would never be able to be employed in their old occupation again. Ninety-eight would require at least six months' rest and treatment before they could be considered fit for work.

Loss of limbs was relatively common among the men. There were 140 cases of amputation, 48 due to shot wounds, 82 due to accidents and 10 due to primary infections. Thirty-eight men were ready to be fitted with artificial limbs straight away. However, the specialists reported that 2 men would need re-training for a different occupation as they had lost both arms and a further 2 men would require another amputation.

Of the prisoners, 259 had been involved in serious accidents that had caused injury, 215 of which had occurred during captivity, and 153 were still severely impaired by the injuries they had suffered. Before being captured, 375 men had suffered shot wounds, but many still required treatment for the damage.

A British staff officer walked through the camp and reported back that, having seen 1,000 of the returning POWs, not one was fit for work. Most of the men wore nothing better than rags, with cloth or sacking wrapped around their feet in place of shoes. Their feet were swollen, their legs like matchsticks. Many could simply walk no further and had to rest in beds until trains were available to take them home.

The prisoners were split into four groups based on their condition and ability to work in the future. Group I consisted of 2,116 men who were considered fit enough to find work within the general labour market immediately. Group II consisted of 1,886 men who were only fit for light or particular work due to loss of limbs or impaired abilities. Group III consisted of 8,194 men who would not be able to work for at least six months due to recovery from illness. Group IIIb consisted of 64 men who were considered permanently disabled.

All of these men had been released by the Russians because they were considered unfit for work, and it is clear some had been fortunate to escape when they did. The majority of the men were suffering from some form of malnutrition, followed by tuberculosis and malaria. The commission had the responsibility of reporting all illnesses to the relevant authorities in the men's home districts so that proper hygienic procedures could be put into place to prevent the spread of disease.

The report showed the stark contrast between the health and wellbeing of men held in Russian prison camps compared to those in British or American camps. There is no doubt that the Germans and Russians treated their respective prisoners badly. Reprisals, poor living conditions and lack of concern were all elements of the terrible conditions the men suffered. No wonder Germans frequently made the effort to find British or American troops to surrender to rather than submit to their Eastern European enemies.

It was felt that the plight of these men should be made public and that reports should be broadcast by the BBC and in the German newspapers.

There was an ironic twist to the tale. In early September a group of well-dressed ex-POWs arrived from Russia carrying communist books and pamphlets. The authorities at Friedland realised the men had been through a Russian 'political school'. An intelligence team took full note of the men's particulars before they were sent home. The report remarked: 'It is interesting to note that the well-dressed and well-fed potential communists arrived in the British zone just before the elections.'[1]

KINDNESS AT CHRISTMAS

With the restrictions on fraternisation reduced, the idea surfaced that certain POWs may be allowed to visit British families at Christmas rather than stay confined to the camps. The Quakers were prominently involved in certain regions in organising such visits, including asking members of their congregations to invite a prisoner home. For the men this was an unexpected and greatly appreciated treat; for the War Office and the government it was another nightmare of red tape and legislation.

The subject was raised in political debates; the Secretary of State for War was asked whether in circumstances where transport was not available the prisoner would be allowed to remain overnight at his host's home. The answer was affirmative. He was then asked whether the 5-mile limitation would still apply to the prisoners. He explained that the restrictions would be relaxed for Christmas Eve and Christmas Day to 100 miles. The end result was that prisoners could leave the camp after 2 p.m. on Christmas Eve and would not have to return until 6 p.m. on Boxing Day.

There were still certain regulations to follow, however. Hosts of prisoners of war had to write their invitation to the camp commandant and needed to state the address or addresses where the prisoner would be accommodated. They had to take full responsibility for ensuring the prisoner did not escape while in their care and also had to pre-pay for their guest's transport if he could not pay for it himself.

For those prisoners who did not receive an invitation, late passes could be issued on Christmas Eve and Christmas Day for them to remain outside of the camp until 1 a.m. on 25 and 26 December. The only exclusions to this were prisoners in the category of C+.

Re-Education

Re-education became an issue towards the end of the war. It began in America and the British quickly saw the necessity of continuing the programme in the UK. The idea was to give the German prisoners a solid grounding in the workings of democracy and British politics in the hope that this might inspire a new Germany free from dictatorship and dreams of world domination.

As the war progressed and drew to its inevitable conclusion, many Germans found their minds turned to concerns about the future. Germany's political system was in tatters; as there was no government it was not even possible for the Allies to negotiate a peace treaty with the country and until very recently there remained none.

National Socialism had clearly failed, and while some harboured the hope that without Hitler the system still might work, to most it was clear a new path had to be forged.

Re-education sounds formal and slightly tyrannical, but it was far from it. All the courses and lectures were non-compulsory and were designed to raise debates and discussions, to get ideas flowing and for men to think for themselves.

Some German officers took an interest in the scheme. For them the future was entirely uncertain as it seemed the German officer class would become obsolete in the new Germany. One German officer approached a British officer in a prison camp and suggested that he, and like-minded Germans, might be able to help in the re-education of the German youth. Understandably the British had reservations about this, but they also realised that something had to be done for the officers. Their biggest fear was that left without a purpose, the officer class would once again turn its attention to world domination in a repetition of the events after 1918.

This was not an unfounded fear. Conversations between some officers, which the British had secretly recorded, revealed that many believed a third world war was a possibility once Germany was back on its feet. It seemed the atrocities and disastrous consequences of the Second World War had done nothing to quench certain officers' desire to form an empire for Germany.

Opening Doors – The WEA

> We have discussed the question of taking POWs in W.E.A. classes. Many of our districts are showing a great eagerness to take this opportunity of spreading ideas of our democratic way of life among the Germans and making some contribution to strengthen their morale and there are quite a lot of useful experiments going on up and down the country.[2]

This was stated in part of a letter from the Workers' Educational Association (WEA). With the war concluding, the general feeling was that if the German POWs could be shown democracy in action they would realise its benefits and this would help to forge a new Germany. There was great fear among both the general public and the government that without intervention Germany could slip back into its old ways and a new Hitler and a new war could happen.

The enthusiasm with which some organisations took to the new idea of re-educating the POWs depended largely on their situation and finances. The WEA would have had regular contact with Germans through their members, who might be working alongside them.

The letter, a circular sent to all district secretaries of the organisation, impressed upon the reader that they should encourage the camps to send men to the classes:

I wonder if you would mind going through the list [of camps] and advising your Branches ... to get in touch with the Camp Commandant and supply a programme of their local activities and to see to what extent they can arrange for groups of Germans who may speak English to attend not only their classes but other functions connected with the Branch.

Arrangements for classes within the camps were also being considered, though it was to be dealt with as a separate matter. The letter concluded: 'I am sure, in spite of the fact we are heavily committed in our normal work, that you will see the immense contributions that we can make to the enlightenment of these men.'

The idealism of the scheme, however, did not fund it and another letter gave a very different view of the difficulties of educating German POWs:

I am greatly worried about the financial aspects of the POW work ... I am sending a circular ... urging our Districts to supply facilities and to admit Prisoners of War to classes, but I am told there are no funds whatever available either for transport for these men or for a nominal payment of a few coppers per lecture towards the cost of local administration, to say nothing of funds for lecturers fees where such lecturers are invited into the camps. It seems to me to be deplorable, if I may say so.

The writer was clearly feeling under pressure from many quarters; he continued:

Only this morning, I have received two letters, one from the Foreign Office, asking us to send 200 sets of free leaflets for distribution to Harvest Camps, and the other asking for posters and pamphlets and free literature for local Labour Exchanges for re-settlement purposes. The latter is nothing to do with the Foreign Office, but these examples will illustrate our difficulties.

A voluntary body, which already last year had a deficit of over £3000 cannot supply the free services of lecturers, publicity material and do the administrative work, particularly for Government Departments and find the money to do it.

However, the advantages of using the WEA classes to educate German POWs were considered to outweigh the financial issues. The London headquarters were going to organise the scheme as 'the work of the W.E.A. can play a very important part not only in making Ps/W [prisoners of war] more valuable citizens on their return to Germany, but also in maintaining good morale in the camps'.

The Foreign Office continued to refuse to be responsible for covering costs of transport to the classes, and they suggested that, while attendance should be free, if a charge had to be made the maximum would be 2s 6d per prisoner for a course lasting six sessions; but if a lecturer was to be invited into the camps to teach, a fee of 1s per prisoner would be permitted to cover costs. Quite clearly the role of the WEA in re-education was considered too important to allow financial problems to get in the way.

'Only One in Ten is Now a Nazi'

Re-educating POWs in the short term was one thing, but the long-term effects of the system were of even greater importance to the authorities. There was also a propaganda element to re-education. The general public were informed of the system in an attempt to make them feel more positive towards Germany and the future. The last thing anyone wanted was talk of Germany building itself back up into a dangerous enemy power.

In the March of 1946 the *Evening Standard* newspaper featured an article about the triumphs of the re-education programme:

> For nearly two years the Political Intelligence Department of the Foreign Office have been working hard to 're-educate' these [Germans]. They are trying to ensure that when they do return to Germany it will not be as unrepentant Nazis, but as men able to become useful citizens of a new Germany.
>
> It is clear today that the imaginative programme of re-education has had a marked effect on their outlook. Only one ex-Wehrmacht man in ten is now officially classified as an unrepentant Nazi. This means that the fervent pro-Nazis have been reduced by one half.[3]

The writer of the article had been to visit the newly opened Wilton Park, an experimental centre where groups of selected prisoners were sent for an intensive six-week course. The first course had been run as a trial and apparently the results had been deemed good enough that further courses were planned. The reporter visited Wilton Park on a weekend during the second course.

The principal of Wilton Park was an Oxford don of German ancestry. He told the paper:

You must understand that in six weeks you can't teach a man very much. These men have been indoctrinated for years, in many cases since childhood, with Nazi and militarist beliefs. Our task is to teach them how to teach themselves – how to use their minds again.

I call it 'pump-priming' and the men are told they must work the pump themselves in order to become intelligent and civilised people.

The school had taken in 320 pupils from a range of POW camps, ranks, ages and military divisions. A third were aged under 25 and had therefore grown up in an entirely Nazi environment, never knowing anything different. In many respects these were the hardest to change as they knew nothing else, while the older men could remember a time before the Nazi party came to power.

Wilton Park was set up like most POW camps, though the courses were run in a deliberately liberal way to encourage independent thought in the men. Every lecture ended with the opportunity for criticism and discussion – for many of the younger men this was a novel experience.

Distinctions of rank were not recognised within Wilton Park. On first arriving German officers would attempt to order privates to carry their luggage, whereupon the principal would tell them, 'You come here to learn, not to be soldiers.'

The reporter was shown a classroom where students were discussing the newly started Nuremberg trials and debating points of international law and its enforcement. The lecturer was a barrister able to explain the legal implications of the trials to the men. The reporter took note of part of the discussion which was led by one blonde-haired young man who remarked: 'I can understand some people being sceptical because the Nuremberg trial is the first of its kind and people might think the verdict has been decided in advance.'

An older man shook his head earnestly and responded: 'No. It is in the interest of the victorious countries to have a fair trial, for they don't wish to make martyrs of the Nazis.'

A dark young man with a scar on his forehead then interposed with an argument for having a permanent international court: 'All decent people, and I would like to include most Germans in that, want it. There must be a start, and if it has to be with Germany, let it be so.'

This comment was viewed with approval and, as the reporter was escorted away, the discussion continued enthusiastically, with one prisoner suggesting the Nuremberg judges owed their loyalty to the world and not any one country.

The overall syllabus of the park tended to focus on the history of Germany, particularly how the troubles that led to the Second World War started before Hitler, even as far back as Bismarck. Most of the men were ignorant of Germany's past. They also studied British institutions and the democratic practices of the country, along with comparing the role of the individual in a free society to the individual's role under a dictatorship.

The park also offered opportunities for the students to join various societies, and the art society in particular became the centre of a peculiar political debate. Some of the society members had painted pictures in a modernist style, a style Hitler would have termed 'degenerate'. Other students when viewing the pictures expressed that they could see nothing in them, at which point one infuriated partisan painter told them, 'Anyone who doesn't like these pictures is a Nazi at heart!'

Troubled by this declaration, the 'Nazi philistines' sought out the principal and asked whether they were really lost souls because they could not understand modern art. The principal had to explain that they were perfectly entitled to their views as long as they were tolerant of those expressed by others.

The camp ran a daily news-sheet organised by a former school teacher from Cologne. He had previously helped to run a newspaper in a POW camp in Yorkshire, which had initially experienced problems caused by the ardent Nazis in the camp, though these were eventually resolved when the Nazis were segregated.

The reporter was also introduced to his assistant, a young man with a talent for watercolours. He showed him some examples: several were pictures of prison camps and of Hamburg, his home town, but one was of Yalta. The principal asked the young man if he had been at the Yalta conference. With a wry smile, the young man shook his head and informed him that he had been to Yalta as part of a victory parade under von Manstein.

Before the war the young man had been part of a Social Democratic party youth organisation. When Hitler took power the society found it necessary to disguise its political motivations by pretending to be a sports club. But the deceit did not last long and eventually the leader was shot and many others sent to prison.

The news-sheet was not the park's only source of information: British dailies were provided for the prisoners, along with the standard POW newspaper that was distributed to all camps across the country. They also had access to news films and had recently seen a newsreel about one of the Nazi concentration camps. This was the only compulsory film ever to be shown to the prisoners and many found the scenes disturbing. Some even tore off their decorations and stamped them into the ground as soon as they left the hut where the film had been shown.

Overall, the students at Wilton Park found the experience enjoyable and mentally stimulating. The men chosen to attend were selected for their intelligence; they were individuals who relished the challenge of learning new information and who had felt stifled in the usual camp environments. They were expected to work hard on the courses which were not designed for luxury. The men's quarters were sparsely furnished and their rations were half that of the British guard, but this seemed to do little to deter the men from avid learning.

The reporter concluded his article with a quote from the principal:

> Of course the true test will be ten years from now when we see what sort of citizens they turn out to be. Perhaps there are one or two clever Nazis here pretending they have been enlightened. It doesn't really matter. The great majority really want to learn and although it is a little early to judge, … I feel convinced that here we are working on the right lines.[4]

While the newspapers revelled in the success of re-education, official reports showed a different story. Firstly, re-education was not compulsory and on the whole those who attended were already in the 'white' or 'grey' band for their political leanings. It was also very difficult to assess just how great an impact the scheme had had on the prisoners and on Germany as a whole. The actual number of men who went on courses was minor considering the size of the German population. Did re-education have more to do with alleviating anxiety in the British public rather than actually changing attitudes among the prisoners and beyond in Germany? The answer is that even when studies were conducted after the war, the extent of re-education's influence was too difficult to determine.

Re-Education Beyond POWs

The whole point of re-education was to enable a new Germany to develop founded on the principles of democracy. Initially, the only Germans who could benefit from the classes were those in POW camps. After 1948, as the final wave of repatriations finished, the British considered spreading their programme wider.

There were large numbers of Germans who did not have the opportunity to attend the classes. This could have been because they did not fight in the war or because they were imprisoned in a different country. And there were those of the old regime who argued that the POWs who had attended courses while in Britain had been the victims of 'political indoctrination' and considered their opinions, therefore, of little value. The British were also interested in reaching out to the female population of Germany.

In response to this, they issued invitations to German citizens to travel to Britain and attend courses at Wilton Park.[5] They hoped that by bringing ordinary citizens over from Germany they might learn about re-settlement and re-orientation ideas, as well as the running of discussion groups, open debate having never been part of the Nazi regime. On their return home they could explain and develop these concepts among their compatriots and dispel the criticism of 'white' POWs, that they were suffering from 'brainwashing'. Finally, it was hoped that their comments might prove to be good publicity for the British.

Responsibility for selecting students fell to the regional HQs in Germany. Candidates needed to be 'young and active as possible', and from a range of regions. The courses and necessary travelling required high levels of mental and physical fitness. The Education Branch felt that these considerations were not being taken seriously enough by those who selected students. In a typed document, they stated that candidates needed to be chosen on their fitness merits, and that the courses were not to be viewed as a reward for virtue, however worthy the student was. Only in special circumstances should a civilian aged over 40 be sent and certainly none aged over 45.

Students came from all walks of life, diversity being key, the British felt. They anticipated that the younger candidates would be interested in the problems of political re-education and tried to ensure that they also included representatives of German organisations. For each course six students were to be representatives of the trade unions, each political party was to send one representative, two were to come from the co-operative societies and four from the land administration. Eight newspaper editors or journalists were individually invited to attend, and nine educational representatives were selected to join the courses. The courses lasted six weeks and included discussion groups on various topics, including 'Germany's development from Bismarck to present', 'information on Britain', 'international civics' and 'the individual and the community'. Practical activities helped to break up the course into manageable chunks.

Tutorials and lectures were included in the material. The subjects for these lectures were usually quite heavy and dealt with social politics, such as 'German internal problems as seen by a military government official', 'British foreign policy', 'the work of the British Council', 'an approach to the study of history', 'the position of the trade unions in England today' or 'co-operative co-partnership'.

There was also a House of Commons Brains Trust with representatives from the Labour, Liberal and Tory parties.

Part of the course involved showing the students the system of re-education used with the POWs. A visit to a POW camp was arranged as well as a visit to the experimental camp where reorientation of politically 'black' Nazi youths was attempted.

Visits to a range of institutions were also organised, though not all students attended every visit and priority was given to those with a professional interest in the place in question. Trips to colleges, schools, co-operative factories, the Houses of Parliament, Fleet Street to talk with journalists, the German service of the BBC, rural district councils, the law courts, the Bureau of Current Affairs and Oxford University were all arranged. Within the training centre there was a library consisting of 3,000 volumes, along with the daily newspapers and certain periodicals.

The Education Branch did not expect the candidates to finance themselves, they were prepared to pay each student £1 in vouchers for their journey and 10s 6d weekly for their 'pocket money'. This enabled students to make one trip a week to London.

Newly arrived candidates were met at Liverpool Street station and taken by coach to Wilton Park. Accommodation was a bedsit room housing two to three students.

The attendance of women on the courses was seen by the British as an experiment. Initially the War Office objected but were eventually persuaded to allow a certain number of female candidates. Out of sixty students on one course, ten were women. These were a sample group; the Education Branch would wait to see how they managed the course before deciding whether more women should be allowed to attend. It was a heavy burden that these ten women carried unknowingly on their shoulders. They were a late selection and, due to the short notice from the Education Branch, it was put in the hands of the German Political Branch and Women's Affairs Section to choose candidates. If the female students did well it was suggested that female German lecturers might be brought to Britain at a later date as well.

Just as the courses were being organised, the War Office abruptly requested that Wilton Park be evacuated of its training staff so it could be used for returning British troops. The result would have been the cancellation of all the courses. Fortunately, the War Office was persuaded to withdraw its request and the next course, destined to begin on 14 January, could continue.

The feeling among the tutors was that, to enable them to successfully conduct their courses and connect with their students, they should be aware of events happening in the British zone of Germany. A telegram was sent to Germany requesting that four tutors pay a short visit to the country, with each tutor given specified areas they would be best to travel to. They would give lectures if required and the visits would be sponsored by the Education Branch of the War Office.

The effect of these courses on the students was, in general, difficult to discern. However, it was noted that on their return home the students were able to join in with discussions and debates with authority due to their time in England – something that previously the German public had been unused to. It was reported they had 'caused general curiosity' and were able to endorse much of what had been said by the 're-educated' POWs, who had previously been treated with scepticism. A comment from a trades union representative who had been on a course was highly encouraging:

> Everybody should experience for himself what we have learned from the democratic institutions and methods and personal relationship of the English population among each other and to the Germans. We were very strongly impressed by the fact that there was no antagonistic feeling against us, although Britain suffers considerably from the aftermath of the war.

Favourable articles were also appearing in the German press, not just concerning the courses, but about the treatment of the POWs in general and camp conditions. Headlines from various articles were upbeat and positive about Britain: 'We set off for a course at Wilton Park', 'British MPs hold discussions with German POWs' and 'When a German arrives in London today'. Press conferences held in Kiel and Hamburg raised similar comments, the visitors expressing their appreciation for the courses and the opportunity to attend, and twice German students spoke on the BBC about their experiences.

There were criticisms, nevertheless, mainly focusing on the complications of administering the courses and organising travelling. Students came from a range of zones and issues arose when permits were not given for candidates to travel. Overnight accommodation before the journey to England was another problem that caused frustration.

Then there were those who would like to learn more about everyday England rather than listen to lectures on British institutions. They wanted more outside visits to learn by direct experience. Another concern was that Germany should be running similar courses to supplement its education system and develop reorientation plans.

There was one final important issue: the influence of the returning candidates depended entirely on what opportunities they were given to speak and discuss what they had seen back in Germany. This was one aspect that the British could have little control over and had to rely on their students' abilities and desire to debate what they had learned openly.

OPERATION SEAGULL[6]

By the end of the war there were around 350,000 POWs in Britain. At the end of 1946 the British began Operation Seagull, the code name for the mass repatriation of its POWs. In the beginning, prisoners were selected for release based on a variety of conditions, from occupation and health to political leanings. It was hoped that by sending back 'white' anti-Nazi prisoners first, the way would be paved for a new democracy and this would be established before the 'black' ardent Nazis were sent home.

However, the organisation of such a scheme was never going to be simple. Aside from choosing which prisoners should go back first, there was the difficulty of 'zones'.

Conditions between zones varied dramatically. While the US and Britain were wary of allowing France to occupy part of Germany due to the age-old animosity between the two nations, it was in fact the Russians who turned their zone into little better than a prison camp for the natives who lived there. Food shortages, corrupt police, constant threats of being sent to concentration camps and the censorship of letters out of the zone meant many people scraped by living in poverty. Some Germans were so terrified of returning to East Germany and the reaction they might face from the Russians that they either escaped from repatriation parties or sought to become British citizens. There seems to have been a certain sympathy among the British authorities for the men's fears. They had witnessed the horrors of the Russian prison camps and must have wondered what life in the Soviet-controlled zone would be like for these men.

But, despite fears and concerns, repatriation had to begin. Between 21 December and 20 January, 5,255 Germans (excluding groups where men were split between multiple zones) were sent back to the British zone; of these, 2,095 were considered anti-Nazi in their views and 1,030 were men employed in essential work (515 timber workers and 515 miners). The French received 1,615 men, 1,100 of which were considered 'white' in their attitudes. The Americans received 1,545 Germans into the US zone, 515 of which were anti-Nazi, and, finally, the Russians received 2,610 men, 1,580 of which were 'whites'.

The prisoners all arrived initially at Cuxhaven and were then transferred by rail to Munsterlager WDC. There they were sorted by address and gradually dispatched to their relevant zones. Those who lived within the British zone could be discharged from Munsterlager, while those living in other zones would be sent in groups on specific dates. A typical list read that 1,000 men would be sent to the French zone on 23 November, another 2,000 would travel to the US zone in two groups on 26 November and 2 December, and 3,000 men destined for the Russian zone would journey by train to their respective regions on 4 and 10 December.

There were other concerns that had to be dealt with prior to repatriation. Special personnel were considered too valuable within the camps to be immediately repatriated. These people included doctors, nurses and dentists. The British authorities were in a quandary; if they sent these men back it would leave a gulf in the camp they could not easily replace. It seems that using British doctors and dentists was not considered, but there were ideas that qualified German civilians might be persuaded to come to Britain and work within the camps if suitable terms could be arranged.

The family arrangements of a repatriated man could be even more complex and were unanticipated by the British authorities. Many men were sent back to their original addresses only to discover their wife and family had been evacuated from or had fled the home during the conflict, and now found themselves trapped in a different zone. The British authorities in Germany were concerned about trying to reunite families, but transferring civilians between zones was not a contingency that had been covered in Operation Seagull's remit.

COMPASSIONATE REPATRIATION

The total number of Germans repatriated as 'compassionate cases' was 19,761. These were prisoners whose families were deemed to be suffering severe hardships which could be alleviated by the early return of the prisoner. It was a British plan that failed to get international backing. The French zone accepted the scheme in principle but never actually acted on it. The Americans refused to have anything to do with it and the Russians never gave any reply. This left only the British zone, but in 1946 things were too chaotic there for compassionate repatriation to work, and POWD (Prisoner of War Department) eventually took over organising the men in February 1947. By the following March the first full batch of men repatriated on compassionate grounds returned to Germany.

The system had been devised after letters were received by various authorities from German families requesting the early release of certain prisoners. Initially there was no means of dealing with these requests. However, when the British government introduced compassionate repatriation, 500 men a month could be sent home in direct response to these letters. To produce a suitable selection 700 applications were examined per quota. The applications were to come from the family stating their relationship to the POW and why he should be sent home early.

Prisoners' applications were judged by a group of six POWs who had been chosen for their integrity, intelligence and maturity. The only criterion for these cases was the hardship suffered by the prisoner's family and the necessity of his early return.

The sad letters from the men's families shine a light on the plight of post-war Germany: 'The wife of Paul Becker, a prisoner since June 1944, had both her legs amputated after an accident in June 1946. He has only one child left, the other having died of starvation in February 1945.'[7]

Another from January 1947 stated:

[Hermann von Kleist Schmenzin's] case was brought to the attention of Mr Pink by Mr Ian Colvin, Berlin correspondent of Kemsley newspapers.

As to the financial position of Frau von Kleist Schmenzin [Hermann's stepmother], she is in possession of a small monthly stipend from two German sources, 'the Victims of Fascism' and 'the Victims of the 20th July'. These together probably amount to not more than 400 marks, so that you will appreciate that with three small children to bring up her lot is far from easy, and it would be a great relief to her to have her stepson home. The majority of her estates and possessions were in the Eastern Zone, so that she has lost all these.

Kleist was in the next draft of men sent back on compassionate grounds. In February 1948 a well-known German lawyer brought another case to the attention of the authorities:

> the speedy repatriation of Georg Renken P/W No. B.266117, No. 246 POW Camp, Basildon House, Basildon, Nr Pangbourne, Berkshire.
>
> … Renken was born on 20 May 1923 and has been held as a POW in England since October 1944. His father is a farmer with a small property at Adolfsdorf, Nr. Rothenburg (Hannover), he is over 60 years of age and is seriously ill with heart and stomach disease and unfit for work. Satisfactory medical evidence has been produced to us in support of these allegations …
>
> The farm property is decaying owing to a lack of adequate labour, all of which is now provided by a 17 year old youth and a petition from the local Bürgermeister has been submitted to us with the application … describing the present parlous condition of the property which, it is stated, can only be saved from ruin by the repatriation of the son, as apparently no other local labour is available.

Unsurprisingly, there were POWs who attempted to manipulate the system to get home sooner. They persuaded their families and even officials into lying for them to ensure their early return. POWD were aware of the problem and conducted spot-checks of POWs to test the validity of their claims.

In September 1947 they determined that out of a group of men being repatriated on compassionate grounds, 55 per cent were entirely justified in their claims, 26 per cent were acceptable and 19 per cent were found to have lied and manipulated the system.

Britain was unique in having compassionate repatriation and the British were proud of it, seeing it as an 'expression of pure humanity without strings'. Among the German prisoners, on the other hand, the resentment of being detained in Britain after the war overshadowed any feelings they had on compassionate repatriation. They used it where they could, and could not complain about it, but on the whole it was a topic not talked about as it did not fit in to the negative group thinking that they were being detained unfairly and unlawfully.

Whatever positive feeling the British government and military authorities had hoped to achieve by their humanity towards their prisoners never materialised. Among the returning Germans compassionate repatriation was rapidly ignored and forgotten, surpassed instead by a national resentment at Britain's tardy return of its prisoners. Yet compassionate repatriation remains a unique Britain creation among the holding powers of the Second World War.

REPATRIATION FEELINGS

It is fair to say that out of all the issues that arose around Britain holding prisoners of war, repatriation was the most contentious one. It was never going to be simple to send home large numbers of men of mixed political leanings, some of whom could potentially still be a risk to the fragile peace Europe found itself enjoying.

Ideally, Germans of either anti-Nazi or non-political views would be sent home first with the hope they could pave the way for the more ardent Nazis who would return afterwards. It was felt that if a functioning democracy could be established before the dangerous elements were sent home then the risk of them rousing support for another war would be minimal.

There were other issues. War criminals needed to be dealt with suitably, and Germany was a divided country; just the logistics of sending men to their correct region was difficult enough, but then consideration had to be made about prisoners of other nationalities who also had to be sent back. Add to the confusion the need to ensure that essential German camp staff were not sent away leaving a gulf in the camp and that Britain was still in desperate need of a suitable skilled workforce that on occasion only German prisoners could provide, and the situation became decidedly messy.

Britain has been largely criticised for its tardiness in sending prisoners home. There were delays, but this was not due to the government wanting 'revenge' on its prisoners, as was the rumour that ran rife in the camps, but down mainly to red tape and organisation. Britain was a country that had suffered severe damage and its first priority was to its own people, to ensure they did not go homeless, that essential facilities were repaired or rebuilt and that the country continued to function. Once repatriation properly began the authorities were sending 15,000 men home each month. This required transport, supplies and staffing, not to mention dealing with the American, French and Russian zone authorities. Hardly an easy task.

Yet, at the same time, it is understandable that POWs and their families back home felt bitter about the length of time it was taking for the men to return to their normal lives.

The British government felt it was trying its best and resented those who criticised their actions. In one report on the subject it was written:

> We feel, however, that it is appreciated neither in Germany nor in the United Kingdom that Great Britain is repatriating its PW probably more quickly than any of the other Allies.
>
> We are surprised to read that PW returning from America made odious comparisons between their situation in the United Kingdom and the situation in the United States. It is certainly more than likely that the morale of PW still in England is lower than it was six months ago.

In fact, the deterioration in morale was due to the method of repatriation rather than the speed. It had always been the case that 'whites' or 'greys' in the prison camps had the strongest morale and often kept the other prisoners' spirits lifted. They were also more inclined to view the British favourably and this affected the other Germans.

With their removal and return to Germany that influence was diminished. Only 'blacks', with their pro-Nazi attitudes, remained and it was then that resentment began to rise. Along with this, the Americans were shipping back the German prisoners that had originally been sent from England at the start of the war. These men had mostly been captured in the early days of the conflict, many of them from U-boats who were ardent Nazis. In America they had been allowed to maintain their Nazism, in some camps even being allowed to salute a German flag and pictures of Hitler. They had retained much of their beliefs in National Socialism, the superiority of the German race and the importance of Germany carving out its own empire. These men were now sent back to camps where morale was low, feelings were mixed and the majority of anti-Nazis had been removed. Their influence, therefore, was entirely negative and created much of the anti-British feelings that started to resurface.

The 'blacks' also resented being categorised, not least because being labelled as 'black' in your political views meant being sent to the bottom of the pile in terms of repatriation. Many denied they were Nazis, or stated they had been misrepresented; those that maintained their views on National Socialism could not understand why their attitudes should mean they returned home last. No doubt some felt that they should in fact be the ones to return home first.

British attitudes varied. Some complained about the speed with which the Germans were being sent home, while others were more concerned with Britain's appearance in the eyes of POWs and their families:

> We are shocked to read that Sir Ralph Glyn asserts that we are doing 'little or nothing in any organised way to see to it that repatriated PW should be full of praise ... and good agents ... for the British way and purpose.' His assertions that they add to the problems created by a discontented German population is true only insofar as we are unable satisfactorily to place them in employment worthy of their intentions.

Repatriation Fears

Escape attempts continued right up until all the German POWs had either been discharged or repatriated. In the latter years of the war escape attempts appeared to increase, which some suggested was due to the use of guards less proficient than previously and the relaxing of restrictions throughout the country. Just after the German surrender there was a sudden lull in escapes, followed by sporadic attempts. There may have been various reasons for this; initially, the German surrender had a knock-on effect on prisoner morale, the reasons for escaping losing some of their point. However, as the process of repatriation slowly began and it became clear that many would not return home soon, some men grew frustrated; they saw other men sent home before them and the process of selection seemed random and unfair. It also appeared that the authorities were less concerned with escapes than they once had been. Notices were sent out to police to let them know if a POW had absconded, but unless the man was considered a real threat, little effort seems to have been made to find them.

There were other reasons as well for escape attempts. Some men could not face repatriation, especially to the Russian zone where conditions were incredibly harsh and people lived in fear of being sent to prison camps for the slightest infringement. There was also fear of reprisals. No wonder some men dreaded returning home.

An example of two such cases appears in a notice from the Metropolitan Police. On 15 November two Germans from a group of thirty-one ex-POWs due to be repatriated on 26 November disappeared. One was named as Guenther Schumacher, 35 years of age, who had previously threatened suicide. He was described as thick set, with grey hair, a pale face, clean-shaven and speaking English.

The second was Rudolph Richarz, aged 28, who spoke English with an American accent. They were both dressed in civilian clothes and previous enquiries as to their whereabouts had proved fruitless.

At least in the initial stages of repatriation the Secretary of State could not force, other than through individual deportation orders, men to be sent home. While in certain cases he would push through a deportation, there was no generalised order and the police could not detain any ex-POW who did not wish to go with a repatriation party. Nor did they have the power to compel a man to return to Germany. When prisoners did abscond from repatriation parties, the matter was simply to be reported to the Home Office and a search made.

REPATRIATION OF OTHER NATIONALITIES

Life would have been simpler if there had only been Germans to worry about repatriating from Britain, but the situation was far more complex than that. During the war Hitler's forces had conscripted men of various nationalities, sometimes forcibly, and these men now had to be dealt with and sent home to their respective countries. But even this was not simple. Borders and boundaries had changed, Poland occupied part of Germany, citizenship was no longer straightforward.

In October 1946 seventeen men discharged from the Polish army demob centre in Scotland arrived at Lustringen transit camp to be repatriated. These men had a convoluted story. Originally the men were German nationals who resided in Poland, or in parts of Germany which Poland occupied after the First World War. They ranked among the German minority and had Polish connections and sympathies.

Relations between Poland and Germany had never been good. Divided up between Russia, Prussia and Austria in the nineteenth century, Poland effectively ceased to exist, until 1918 when the collapse of the Russian, Austro-Hungarian and German monarchies and the Treaty of Versailles returned Poland to the map. The establishing of Poland as a republic was enthusiastically rejoiced by its nationals and Polish patriotism strengthened. However, Germany was unhappy at seeing some of its German-speaking territories becoming redefined as parts of Poland.

Few can forget that on 1 September 1939 the Nazi invasion of Poland marked the start of another epic conflict. The Polish leadership was 'liquidated'. Jews, politicians and intellectuals found themselves being sent to Nazi death camps and eventual extermination.

Germans with Polish connections were still conscripted into the army; for some the only other choice may have been death, but they were far from comfortable serving their enemy.

The seventeen men who had arrived at Lustringen had served in the German army and as a result had become German POWs. While being held in France they were offered and accepted the chance to serve in the Polish army and were sent to join the other Polish forces in Britain. They remained in the Polish army until October 1946 when they were demobilised and repatriated.

The men were technically German, however, and while some were eligible to return to Poland, most were to stay in Germany. As it turned out, all seventeen wanted to remain in Germany and this was agreed as long as they realised that after their fifty-six days of demob leave they had to report to the German authorities and register as ordinary civilians, and that their service in the Polish army did not entitle them to any preferential treatment.

GERMAN ATTITUDES TO THE BRITISH

With Germany war-weary and defeated, its POWs still held in England found themselves staring at an uncertain future. Re-education was just one way of showing the Germans how a democratic and tolerant country might function successfully. Contact with the general population and examples of the way the system worked was another way of demonstrating the benefits of the British way of life.

The German POWs, however, put their own slant on war politics. Isolated in the main from the local populace and desperate for their return home, the men's view of Britain took on unexpected aspects.

Reading material was available in the camps, though popular books often had a lengthy waiting list. Books about the British empire and its methods of governing were eagerly read by the higher-ranking Germans who were trying to develop an understanding of the nation that had conquered them. A theme that was noted among the generals was the idea that 'world politics [was] a game of grab with the British regarded as the most successful grabbers'. This elicited envy and also admiration among the generals.

There was also much respect for the British empire. From the books they read, the Germans were struck by the seeming respect the British received from their native subjects and how they could govern such large expanses with relatively few people. They believed for Germany to achieve a similar empire they would have to deploy a far greater number of people to govern their different territories and would require a vast secret service.

There were other reasons for German admiration of the British. With the Russians breathing down their necks, it was felt that the British could present Germany with its only hope of protection from complete Russian domination. Thoughts were turning to future conflicts, and the feeling was that World War III would be a struggle between Western capitalism and Eastern communism. The German officers felt that their own and their country's only chance of survival was to side with the UK and face the Russians together.

Other views were raised between the German officers and the British camp staff. General Thoma spoke to a British officer and said that if the UK did not get in first then Germany would have to side with Russia, which would only disadvantage the British. He explained his country only had two options, to look west or east.

However, while these views were voiced to the camp staff in private conversations which the British recorded in secret, the German officers said nothing publicly about the possibility of joining with Russia. Many felt such a move would render them obsolete.

After the Moscow conference of 1944 a wave of depression hit the officer-class prisoners and Thoma was greatly affected. The idea that England and America could be 'played off' against Russia finally seemed to be finished. Some still hoped that the unresolved issues of Poland would lead to contention between the Allies. The final nail in the coffin was news that Austria would be separated from Germany – this seemed to indicate that the Allies intended to carve up Germany, 'cutting off South Germany along the line of the Main'. This information brought increased despair as such division, it was felt, would leave Germany an impotent power.

The feeling that the peace terms were hugely detrimental to Germany led to the reverse of earlier desires for surrender. Now some Germans considered the only option was to fight on; the defeat was inevitable but it seemed the only way to continue.

ANTI-NAZI FEELING AND WAR CRIMES

The failure of the war led to many generals condemning the party they had once served. All the disasters of the conflict and Germany's future troubles were to be blamed on the Nazi party and Hitler. He had proved a failure and a fool. While the feeling was not unanimous and was more prominent among the higher ranks than ordinary soldiers, anti-Nazism was becoming stronger.

Hitler was beginning to be viewed as an obsessive, conceited man, incapable of war strategies and wasteful of both materials and his men's lives. His refusal to let Rommel evacuate from Africa in 1943, and his obstinacy at holding on to the Crimea, were given as just two examples of his incompetence.

Hitler's political acumen was criticised as well: he was blamed for starting the war too early and for choosing to attack Russia, which, according to General Thoma, lost them the war. Talk that Hitler only listened to his 'yes-men' had, in the past, led to discussion among the General Staff about an overthrow of the Nazi party. But, speaking to the British officers within the camp, the generals gave clear reasons why such an attack could never have worked, from possible leaders of the revolt being too old, to the scattering of the army, the Nazification of the younger men, the lack of political training among the officers and the fear that spies were everywhere – the reasons for doing nothing outweighed everything else. It was also felt that little would be gained from such a move.

After the Moscow conference and the news that men suspected of war crimes would be placed on trial, the feeling among the German officers was both one of fear and outrage. Some of the generals began spreading counter-propaganda around the camps, saying the Prussians 'have seriously attempted to deny their Fatherland'; while others believed they would be held for eighteen months after the end of the war while their pasts were examined.

It was a popular stance among the generals to convince themselves that no real war crimes had been committed, other than by the Gestapo and SS troops. They maintained that any people they had shot had been justified as it was for espionage or sabotage, and while they confessed to the shooting of hostages, two generals, Armin and Cruewell, expressed distaste for the practice but had to do it under military law. General Thoma defended the practice as the only means of dealing with sabotage or the murdering of German troops in occupied countries.

While there were those who spoke of the way Germany had behaved as appalling and that it had proved incapable of governing itself, others worked tirelessly to justify or disbelieve the crimes being presented.

No Escape

It is a commonly held belief that no prisoner of war ever escaped the clutches of their British captors. Attempted escapes were made but the men were quickly found, so it is said. Britain supposedly had an unparalleled record for retaining all its POWs.

While this may have been the popular view presented by the media and propaganda to reassure a population that had to live in close quarters with the enemy, official records reveal a different story. In 1949 there were still German POW fugitives living in Britain. They had escaped from either camps or hostels and had not been repatriated. Some had no desire to return to Germany, others had disappeared and were yet to be found. In an official document dated 3 March 1949 it was stated that sixty-three POWs remained at large. With the war over, this presented a difficult administrative problem.

Initially, the Aliens Department agreed to deal with any of these POWs if they were recaptured by means of deportation. But the agreement soon came into question and the department's legal advisors decided that it was not appropriate for prisoners of war to be deported; instead they had to be repatriated.

The Aliens Department felt it unsuitable to ask the police to detain and hold recaptured POWs, nor could they be expected to escort the men to ports for return to their own country. Instead, the department handed responsibility back to the War Office and they resumed their wartime arrangements with the police, whereby any prisoner of war handed to the police was to be turned over immediately to the nearest military authority. The War Office would deal with them thereafter.

Circulars were prepared, as were lists of the escaped prisoners, though the War Office did state: 'it may be that many of them have succeeded in leaving the United Kingdom altogether.'

This indeed was the case, as proved by two POWs who had escaped from a camp in Oldham and were recaptured in Germany eighty-three days later. The information on the situation was hazy, but the men had apparently disappeared from their camp in German uniform; it was unclear if they spoke English or how they had got to Germany, yet somehow they had, dispelling the idea that no POW ever escaped British soil.

No precedent existed for dealing with escaped POWs after the war and once repatriation had ended. An exhaustive search was made of the previous regulations and circulars issued during the war, but these mainly dealt with the handling of enemy parachutists or those coming ashore from a submarine, not escaped prisoners who had been at large for some time. Entirely new arrangements needed to be prepared.

The list of escapees showed that the majority vanished after the war ended and repatriation began, the earliest being September 1945. Their reasons for escape would probably have been manifold – some would have detested the length of time the repatriations were taking, aiming to get home sooner by other methods, while others would have wanted to stay in Britain, perhaps having no family to return to, and post-war Germany was not the country they had left behind. Unemployment, shortages and poverty were a mainstay and for some the temptation to stay in England or escape to another country would have been too strong. The prisoners were listed in order of their escape:

P. Van Belligen (army), V. Grun (army), F. Fuchs (M/N), G. Woif (army), K. Rehaag (army), H. Lieberam (army), H. Heidak (GAF), O. Reuter (army), L. Dalderup (army), Steinhauser (navy), A. Schneider (army), E. Kindler (army), W. Borrmann (army), F. Goernardt (army), F. Irmer (army), R. Lauer (army), H. Brandes (army), K.M. Strawe (army), A. Voellings (army), G. Freitag (GAF), F. Konig (army), H. Berner (GAF), F. Speh (army), H.J. Brammar (army), H. Katewitz (army), E. Schmidt (army), H. Muller (GAF), A. Schmidt (GAF), F. Jentsch (navy), F. Gosch (navy), H. Rosen (army), K. Fabiny (army), G. Tacke (GAF), E. Witzel (army), B. Rach (navy), R. Briesemeister (army), C. Sauer (navy), W. Schulz (GAF), H. Dorrl (GAF), H. Roedler (GAF), A. Weichelt (GAF), K. Shanklies (navy), E. Stricharz (GAF), W. Kraemer (GAF), J. Pattermann (GAF), Mittelsorf-Subrirana (GAF), P. Uhrich (GAF), E. Kampman (army), Brochhagen (army), N.G. Hein (army), M. Besch (army), J. Mueller (GAF), E. Kah (army), H. Uhlirsch (army), H. Fritsch (army), W. Fraedrich (SS).

FOND MEMORIES

Some Germans and Italians returned home with such strong feelings about the places and people they had met in Britain that many wished they could have stayed there. Such was the case for SS man Heinrich Steinmeyer, who, as a member of one of Hitler's most feared units, did not expect kind treatment at the hands of the British but was to be surprised.

Steinmeyer had been brought up under Hitler's regime and had joined the Hitler Youth. From there he was recruited to the SS Panzer division in 1944 and saw action at Normandy. After fighting the Americans at the

Battle of the Bulge and then the Red Army, his unit withdrew to Austria, where eventually they surrendered in 1945.

Steinmeyer was held in the camp at Comrie, the same camp where Rosterg met his untimely death, and where ardent Nazis were held because it was considered difficult to escape from. Adolf Hitler's deputy, Rudolf Hess, had even been held there after he crashed his plane in Scotland. As an SS man it was the logical place for Steinmeyer. But while the authorities were concerned about Nazi rebellions, the local residents were more concerned with ensuring the men were welcomed into the community. Steinmeyer was amazed by the kindness he was shown; locals even sent parcels to his mother in Germany when they heard she had fallen ill.

Compared to the battlefields of France, the camp at Comrie was like a holiday to Steinmeyer; he was struck by the beauty of the area and the friendliness of the residents. It was a relief to escape the war. Looking around at the black hillsides, Steinmeyer wondered: 'Why have I been fighting this war?' He fell in love with Scotland so much that after the war he remained in Comrie for seven years, having discovered his hometown was now part of Poland. He eventually returned to Delmenhorst, Bremen.

Steinmeyer became known as 'Heinz' in the village and over the decades he returned several times, making particular friends with five families who came to know him as 'Uncle Heinz' and who regularly received gifts from him. Despite making no secret of his Nazi past, Steinmeyer became part of the community.

At the age of 84 Steinmeyer made the decision that after his death all his life savings and his home, a sum totalling £450,000, was to be left to the elderly residents of Comrie. His ashes were to be scattered at Cultybraggan where the camp was situated.

Conclusion

The story of prisoners of war held by the British has been almost ignored in the annals of Second World War history, yet it is a key part of the war and affected many lives. While this situation caused problems, both logistical and emotional, and although there were skirmishes, arguments and minor conflicts, compared to the treatment of POWs in other countries the British showed a great deal of tolerance for their unusual neighbours.

The social aspect of housing enemy soldiers on British soil was a constant difficulty. Differences of opinion as well as jealousy and even anger could cause fights. But in general the British chose to voice their outrages in the press rather than resort to direct violence. There were also those areas where the POWs were treated as long-lost friends and encouraged to socialise with the locals.

While POWs experienced a mixed bag of reactions from the communities they were housed in, for many the fears of reprisals and hatred they had assumed would greet them were unfounded. The friendships formed during their long stay in Britain encouraged many to remain there long after the war ended.

This presents a very different aspect of the war to what is usually recorded in the history books, but it is one that sums up the wartime spirit of the British, who could look beyond the conflict to the men behind the uniforms and were often prepared to call them friends.

NOTES

1 Ex-Wehrmacht discharged in Russia or the Russian occupied zone of Germany, Zonal Executive Offices, 23 September 1946.
2 The Workers' Educational Association papers in relation to German POWs. The National Archives, Kew. FO 938/298.
3 John Thompson, *Evening Standard*, 13 March 1946.
4 Ibid.
5 Wilton Park Courses. The National Archives, Kew. FO 1032/1095.
6 Operation Seagull. The National Archives, Kew. FO 1052/384.
7 Henry Faulk, *Group Captives*, Chatto and Windus, 1977.

appendix

POW CAMP DIRECTORY

This list is based on official records for the classification of POW camps in Britain. The camps would not necessarily have been in operation all at the same time and earlier numbers were reused for different locations. Camps would also sometimes change number if they changed status. This list cannot be considered comprehensive, as temporary or minor transit camps were not recorded or registered with a specific number under official military documents.

Northern England

Camp No	Location
1	Grizedale Hall, Cumbria
2	Glen Mill, Oldham, Lancashire
4	Windlestone Hall camp, County Durham
4	Gilling camp, Yorkshire
6	Racecourse camp, Doncaster, Yorkshire
8	Warth Mills, Bury, Lancashire
9	Warth Mills, Bury, Lancashire
11	Racecourse camp, York, Yorkshire
12a	Warth Mills, Bury, Lancashire
13	Shap Wells camp, Cumberland
15	Shap Wells camp, Cumberland
17	Lodge Moor camp, Sheffield, Yorkshire
18	Featherstone Park camp, Northumberland
20	Bramham No 1 camp, Yorkshire
29	Ormskirk, Lancashire
36	Walworth Castle, County Durham
50	Garswood Park, Ashton-in-Makerfield, Lancashire
51	Allington, Grantham, Lancashire
53	Sandbeds camp, Brayton, Yorkshire
60	Overdale camp, Skipton, Yorkshire
65	Bank Hall, Preston, Lancashire

69	Darras Hill, Ponteland, Northumberland
73	Storwood camp, Cottingwith, Yorkshire
76	Merry Thought camp, Calthwaite, Cumberland
83	Eden camp, Malton, Yorkshire
91	Post Hill camp, Leeds, Yorkshire
93	Harperley camp, Crook, County Durham
93a	Oaklands Emergency Hospital, Bishop Auckland, County Durham
103	Moota camp, Cockermouth, Cumberland
104	Beela River, Milnthorpe, Westmorland
105	Wooler camp, Northumberland
105	Hetton House camp, Wooler, Northumberland
108	Thirkleby camp, Little Thirkleby, Yorkshire
121	Scriven Hall camp, Scriven Knaresborough, Yorkshire
121	Racecourse camp, Ripon, Yorkshire
126	Melland camp, Manchester, Lancashire
127	Potter's Hill, Sheffield, Yorkshire
136	High Hall camp, Beverley, Yorkshire
136a	Welton House, Brough, Yorkshire
139	Wolviston Hall, Billingham, County Durham
139b	Coxhoe Hall camp, County Durham
146	Newton camp, Kirkham, Lancashire
155	Hornby Hall camp, Brougham, Cumberland
159	Butterwick camp, Boythorpe, Yorkshire
162	Military Hospital, Naburn, York, Yorkshire
163	Butterwick camp, Boythorpe, Yorkshire
164	Weston Lane camp, Otley, Yorkshire
168	Brookmill camp, Woodlands, Kirkham, Lancashire
171	Camp A, Knowsley Park, Prescott, Lancashire
172	Dog and Duck Cottage, Norton-in-Malton, Yorkshire
176	Glen Mill, Wellyhole Street, Oldham, Lancashire
177	Warth Mills, Bury, Lancashire
178	Urebank camp (Ure Bank), Ripon, Yorkshire
211	Knaresborough, Yorkshire
244	Butterwick camp, Malton, Yorkshire
244/245	Butcher Hill, Horsforth, Leeds, Yorkshire
245	Weston Lane camp, Otley, Yorkshire
247	Urebank camp (Ure Bank), Ripon, Yorkshire
248	Norton camp, Cinderhill Lane, Norton, Yorkshire
250	Eden camp, Old Malton, Malton, Yorkshire
250	Thorpe Hall, Rudston, Yorkshire
264	Welton House, Welton, Brough, Yorkshire
283	WD camp, Ledsham Hall, Ledsham
288	Gilling camp, Hartforth Grange, Hartforth Lane, Gilling, Yorkshire
290	Penketh Hostel, South Lane Farm, South Lane, Barrow's Green, Lancashire
291	Kitty Brewster Farm, Blyth, Northumberland
296	Potter's Hill, High Green, Sheffield, Yorkshire

296	Ravensfield Park camp, Rotherham, Yorkshire
296a	Racecourse camp, Doncaster, Yorkshire
564	Stable Road camp, Barlow, Yorkshire
585	Searchlight Site camp, Husthwaite, Easingwold, Yorkshire
605	West Bolden camp, Down Hill Quarry, Sunderland, County Durham
613	Blackbeck camp, Stainton, County Durham
631	Stadium camp, Catterick, Yorkshire
635	Lord Mayor's camp, Amble, Northumberland
636	Cowick Hall, West Cowick, Snaith, Yorkshire
637	Centenary Road, Goole, Yorkshire
662	Stadium camp, Catterick, Yorkshire
664	Stadium camp, Catterick, Yorkshire
667	Byrness camp, Redesdale, Otterburn, Northumberland
678	Fort Crosby, Sniggery Farm, Hightown, Lancashire
690	Thomas Street camp, Selby, Yorkshire
691	Cowick Hall, West Cowick, Snaith, Yorkshire
692	No 4 camp, Longton, Carlisle, Cumberland
696	Warwick camp, Duranhill Road, Carlisle, Cumberland
699	Tyne J. camp, Gosforth, Newcastle-upon-Tyne, Northumberland
1007	No 14 Armoured Fighting Vehicle Depot (AFVD), Burn, Selby, Yorkshire
1015	Station Road, Tadcaster, Yorkshire

Midlands

Camp No	Location
2	Toft Hall camp, Knutsford, Cheshire
4	Scraptoft camp, Leicester
6	Long Marston camp, Warwickshire
8	Mile House, Oswestry, Shropshire
9	Quorn camp, Leicestershire
10	Stamford camp, Lincolnshire
13	The Hayes, Swanwick, Derbyshire
16	Prees Heath, Shropshire
16	Flaxley Green camp, Rugeley, Staffordshire
23	Greenfields camp, Shrewsbury, Shropshire
23	Sudbury camp, Derbyshire
24	No 4 General Hospital (military), Knutsford, Cheshire
25	Cloister Croft camp, Leamington Spa, Warwickshire
27	Ledbury camp, Herefordshire
27	3 Magdala Road, Nottingham
28	Garendon Park, Loughborough, Leicestershire
28	Knightthorpe camp, Loughborough, Leicestershire
31	Ettington Park camp, Warwickshire
34	Acksea camp, Oswestry, Shropshire
35	Boughton Park camp, Boughton, Northamptonshire
39	Castle camp, Warwickshire
49	Farndon Road camp, Market Harborough, Leicestershire

52	Nether Headon camp, East Retford, Lincolnshire
54	Longbridge camp, Droitwich, Worcestershire
58	The Hayes, Swanwick, Derbyshire
58	Nether Heage camp, Belper, Derbyshire
71	Sheriffhales camp, Shifnal, Shropshire
74	Racecourse camp, Tarporley, Cheshire
79	Moorby camp, Ravensby, Lincolnshire
80	Horbling, Sleaford, Lincolnshire
81	Pingley Farm camp, Brigg, Lincolnshire
82	Hempton Green camp, Fakenham, Norfolk
84	Sheet camp, Ludlow, Shropshire
87	Byfield camp, Daventry, Northamptonshire
94	Gaullby Road, Billesdon, Leicestershire
96	Wolseley Road camp, Rugeley, Staffordshire
97	Birdingbury, Bourton-on-Dunsmore, Warwickshire
98	Hill Farm Estate, Addington, Northamptonshire
99	Shugborough Park Hospital, Great Haywood, Staffordshire
100	St Martins camp, Gobowen, Shropshire
106	Stanmford camp, Stanmford, Lincolnshire
131	Uplands camp, Diss, Norfolk
132	Kimberley Park, Kimberly, Norfolk
134	Loxley Hall, Uttoxeter, Staffordshire
138	The Rectory camp, Bassingham, Lincolnshire
140	Racecourse camp, Warwick, Warwickshire
143	Serlby Hall camp, Blyth, Nottinghamshire
147	Boar's Head camp, Nantwich, Cheshire
148	Castlethorpe camp, Brigg, Lincolnshire
151	Pendeford Hall, Wolverhampton, Staffordshire
151a	Lawn camp, Coven, Staffordshire
151b	Halfpenny green, Wolverhampton, Staffordshire
152	Old Liberal Club, Shepshed, Leicestershire
153	Fulney Park, Spalding, Lincolnshire
156	Heath camp, Wellingore, Lincolnshire
166	Wollaton Park camp, Wollaton Hall, Nottingham, Nottinghamshire
167	Shady Lane, Stoughton, Leicester, Leicestershire
169	Tollerton Hall camp, Tollerton, Nottinghamshire
170	Weelsby camp, Grimsby, Lincolnshire
174	Norton camp, Cuckney, Mansfield, Nottinghamshire
175	Flaxley Green camp, Stilecop Field, Rugeley, Staffordshire
179	The Hayes, Swanwick, Derbyshire
180	Marbury Hall camp, Marbury, Northwich, Cheshire
181	Carburton camp, Youngrough Breck, Nottinghamshire
183	Quorn camp, Wood Lane, Quorn (Quorndon), Leicestershire
189	Dunham Park camp, Dunham New Park, Altringham, Cheshire
191	Crewe Hall, Stowford, Crewe, Cheshire
192	Adderley Hall, Adderley, Market Drayton, Shropshire
193	Madeley Tile Works camp, Madeley, Crewe, Cheshire

651	South camp, Donnington, Wellington, Shropshire
656	Boughton camp, New Ollerton, Nottinghamshire
659	South camp, Donnington, Wellington, Shropshire
659	North camp, Donnington, Wellington, Shropshire
665	South Littleton, Evesham, Worcestershire
667/667a	Stoneleigh camp, Stoneleigh, Coventry, Warwickshire
679	83 Ordnance Supply Depot (O.S.D.) (Don), Soulton Road, Shropshire
685	No 3 camp, ESCD, Long Marston, Warwickshire
686	German Prisoner Working Company (GPW Herefordshire), Moreton-on-Lugg
689	Blackmore camp, Blackmore Park, Great Malvern, Worcestershire
702	Kingscliffe (King's Cliffe), Peterborough, Northamptonshire
1004	No 1 camp, Oaks Green, Sudbury, Derbyshire
1004	E' camp, Donnington, Wellington, Shropshire
1005	Barby camp, Willoughby, Rugby, Warwickshire
1008	Allerton camp, Alvaston, Derby, Derbyshire
1010	Weedon camp, Weedon Beck, Northamptonshire
1012	Canwick camp, Canwick, Lincoln, Lincolnshire
1018	Acksea camp, Kinnerley, Oswestry, Shropshire
1023	Sudbury camp, Oaks Green, Sudbury, Derbyshire

Southern Counties

Camp No	Location
6a	Ashton Court, Somerset
7	Winter Quarter camp, Ascot, Berkshire
9	Kempton Park camp, Surrey
10	Cockfosters camp, Middlesex
11a	Trent Park camp, Middlesex
11a	Rayner's Lane, Harrow-on-the-Hill, Middlesex
17	22 Hyde Park Gardens, London
20	Bickham camp, Yelverton, Devon
20	Wilton Park, Beaconsfield, Buckinghamshire
23	Le Marchant camp, Devizes, Wiltshire
23	Kingwood, Godalming, Surrey
25	Lodge Farm camp, Newbury, Berkshire
26	Barton Field camp, Ely, Cambridgeshire
29	Royston Heath camp, Royston, Hertfordshire
30	Carpenter's Road camp, London
30	Anglesey House, Aldershot, Hampshire
32	Wormwood Scrubs, London
33	Old Windmills camp, Blackthorn, Oxfordshire
33	Dancers Hill, South Mimms, Hertfordshire
33	St Martin's Plain, Folkestone, Kent
36	Hartwell Dog Track camp, Aylesbury, Buckinghamshire
37	Sudeley Castle camp, Gloucestershire
37	Colley Lane, Bridgewater, Somerset
40	Somerhill camp, Tonbridge, Kent
41	Ganger camp, Romsey, Hampshire

42	Exhibition Field camp, Holsworthy, Devon
43	Harcourt Hill camp, North Hinksey, Oxfordshire
44	Goathurst camp, Bridgewater, Somerset
45	Trumpington camp, Trumpington, Cambridgeshire
46	Kingsfold camp, Billinghurst, Sussex
47	Motcombe Park camp, Shatesbury, Dorset
55	Shalstone camp, Shalstone, Buckinghamshire
56	Botesdale, Diss, Suffolk
57	Merrow Down camp, Guilford, Surrey
59	Sawtry camp, Sawtry, Huntingdonshire (Cambridgeshire)
61	Wynolls Hill, Coleford, Gloucestershire
65	Setley Plain, Brockenhurst, Hampshire
71	Lower Hare Park, Newmarket, Cambridgeshire
72	Ducks Cross camp, Dacca Farm, Wilden, Bedfordshire
76	Dymond's Farm, Exeter, Devon
78	High Garrett camp, Braintree, Essex
85	Victoria camp, Mildenhall, Suffolk
86	Stanhope camp, Kent
86a	Woodchurch camp, Ashford, Kent
88	Mortimer camp, Berkshire
89	Easton Grey camp, Malmesbury, Wiltshire
90	Friday Bridge, Wisbeach, Cambridgeshire
92	Bampton Road camp, Tiverton, Devon
95	Batford camp, Harpendon, Hertfordshire
107	Penleigh camp, Wookey Hole, Somerset
114	Eden Vale camp, Westbury, Wiltshire
115	White Cross camp, St Columb Major, Cornwall
116	Mill Lane camp, Hatfield Heath, Essex
117	Walderslade camp, Chatham, Kent
122	Rayner's Lane camp, Harrow-on-the-Hill, Middlesex
122	Oxhey Lane camp, Uxbridge road, Middlesex
124	Wapley camp, Bristol, Gloucestershire
124/124a	Ashtongate camp/Bedminster camp, Bristol, Gloucestershire
125	Newlands House, London
128	Meesdon, Hertfordshire
129	Ashford camp, Halstead, Essex
130	West Fen Militia camp, Ely, Cambridgeshire
132	Northwick Park Hospital, Blockley, Gloucestershire
135	Stanbury House camp, Reading, Berkshire
137	Chaddlewood camp, Plympton, Devon
137	Hazeldene camp, Plymstock, Devon
137b	Winsford Tower camp, Beaworthy, Devon
141	Beeson House camp, St Neots, Huntingdonshire (Cambridgeshire)
144	Ruskin Avenue, Kew, Surrey
145	Normanhurst camp, Battle, Sussex
154	Ministry of Works camp, Swanscombe, Kent
157	Bourton camp, Bourton-on-the-Hill, Gloucestershire

160	Military Hospital, Lydiard Park, Purton, Wiltshire
171	Bungay Base camp, Bugay, Beccles, Suffolk
180	Trumpington camp, Trumpington, Cambridgeshire
180	Radwinter North camp, Radwinter Manor, Walden Road, Radwinter, Essex
183	Beckton Marshes camp, East Ham, London
185	Springhill Lodge camp, Five Mile Drive, Blockley, Gloucestershire
186	Berechurch Hall camp, Colchester, Essex
187	Ivybridge camp, Ivybridge, Devon
193	Hampton Park, London
231	Redgrave Park Hospital, Diss, Suffolk
233	Summer House, Ravensbourne, Bromley, Kent
235	Gorhambury Park, Hemel Hempstead, Hertfordshire
235	The Arches, Felden, Hemel Hempstead, Hertfordshire
236	White House, Church Hill, Loughton, Essex
237	Co-Ed-Bel camp, Lubbock Road, Chislehurst, Kent
238	Brook House, Hammingden Lane, Ardingly, Sussex (West Sussex)
239	Westonacres camp, Woodmansterne, Banstead, Surrey
246	Basildon House, Lower Basildon, Pangbourne ,Berkshire
246	North camp, Nettlebed, Henley-on-Thames, Oxfordshire
251	East Cams camp, Portchester Road, Hampshire
257	Pennygillam Farm camp, Launceston, Cornwall
261	W.D. camp, Ampthill, Bedfordshire
263	Leckhampton Court camp, Leckhampton, Cheltenham, Gloucestershire
266	Hutted camp, Bentley Fam, Old Church Hill, Langdon Hills, Essex
267	Mereworth Castle, Mereworth, Waterinbury, Kent
268	Norduck Farm, Aston Abbotts, Buckinghamshire
269	Mansion Potton camp, Potton, Sandy, Bedfordshire
270	Luton Airport camp, Luton, Bedfordshire
273	Flixton Airfield, Flixton, Bungay, Suffolk
273/273a	Debach Airfield, Debach, Woodbridge, Suffolk
274	Ministry of Works camp, Uxbridge Road, Hatch End, Middlesex
275	Topsite camp, Thames, Ditton, Surrey
276/276a	Nissen (Nisson) Creek, Pinhoe, Exeter, Devon
278	WD camp, Clapham, Bedford, Bedfordshire
279	Militia camp, Yaxley Farcet, Huntingdonshire (Cambridgeshire)
282	Brissenden Green camp, Brissenden, Ashchurch, Kent
282	Honghorst House, Woodchurch, Ashford, Kent
286	Purfleet camp, Beacon Hill, Purfleet, Essex
289	Lydiard House, Lydiard Millicent, Swindon, Wiltshire
294	Fisher's camp, Theddon Grange, Alton, Hampshire
295	Cattistock camp, Cattistock, Maiden Newton, Dorset
300	Wilton Park, Beaconsfield, Buckinghamshire
402	Lopscombe Corner camp, Salisbury, Wiltshire
402a	Camp C19, The Avenue, Southampton Common, Southampton, Hampshire

403	Brockley camp, Brockley, Somerset
404	Ivybridge camp, Ivybridge, Devon
405	Barwick House camp, Barwick, Yeovil, Somerset
406	Scarnecross camp, Launceston, Cornwall
410	Le Marchant camp, Devizes, Wiltshire
411	The Wynches camp, Much Hadham, Hertfordshire
553	Bolero camp, Graven Hill, Bicester, Oxfordshire
561	Old Woodbury Hall, Gamlingay, Sandy, Bedfordshire
562	Osterley Park camp, Wyke Green, Isleworth, Middlesex
575	Church Farm, Marston Moretaine, Bedford, Bedfordshire
584	Carfax Estate, Tongham, Hampshire
598	Country House Hotel, Sidford, Sidmouth, Devon
607	Hutted camp, Ickleton Grange, Ickleton, Essex
611	Harrold Hall, Harrold, Bedfordshire
614	Stoneham camp, Eastleigh, Hampshire
624	Ossemsley Manor, Ossemsley, New Milton, Hampshire
628	Hutted camp, Sutton Park, Potton, Bedfordshire
629	Mabledon Park, Tonbridge, Kent
631	Seafield School, Cooden Down, Bexhill, Sussex
632	Arena Road camp, Tidworth, Hampshire
632	Old Windmills camp, Blackthorn, Arncot, Oxfordshire
633	Haig Lines, Crookham, Hampshire
638	Stratton Factory camp, Swindon, Wiltshire
644	Hutted camp, Houghton Conquest, Bedford, Bedfordshire
645	Quarr House, Sway, Lymington, Hampshire
652	Durnell's Farm camp (Magazine Camp), Central Ordnance Depot, Didcot, Berkshire
653	Old Windmills camp, Blackthorn, Arncot, Oxfordshire
654	No 4 Transit camp, Beacon Hill, Purfleet, Essex
654a	RE Bridging camp, Wouldham, Rochester, Kent
655	No 1 Transit camp, Beacon Hill, Purfleet, Essex
657	No 9 Tented camp, Arncott, Bicester, Oxfordshire
657	Shed D35, Graven Hill, Arncott, Bicester, Oxfordshire
658	Barn House Farm, Shipley, Horsham, Surrey
658	Hill camp, Westbury, Wiltshire
661a	Eynsham Park, Eynsham, North Leigh, Oxfordshire
663	Park House 'A', Shipton Bellinger, Tidworth, Hampshire
665	Cross Keys camp, Norton Fitzwarren, Somerset
666	Stoberry Park, Wells, Somerset
668	Aliwell Barracks, North Tidworth, Wiltshire
669	West Ridge camp, Greenford, Middlesex
669	Cruwys Morchard, Tiverton, Devon
670	St Radigrund's camp, Dover, Kent
670a	St Martin's Plain, Shorncliffe Camp, Folkestone, Kent
670b	Shatesbury camp, Dovercourt, Harwich, Essex
671	Popham camp, Micheldever, Winchester, Hampshire
672	Fargo camp, Larkhill, Salisbury, Hampshire

673	Bridestow, Okehampton, Devon
673	Home Park camp, Plymouth, Devon
674	Stratton Factory camp, Swindon, Wiltshire
674	Consols Mine camp, Tywardreath, Par Cornwall
674/675	Old Dean Common camp, Camberley, Surrey
675	Hiltingury Road, Chandler's Ford, Eastleigh, Hampshire
676	Puckridge camp, Fleet Road, Aldershot, Hampshire
680	Shaftsbury camp, Dovercourt, Harwich, Essex
681	Osterley Park camp, Wyke Green, Isleworth, Middlesex
681/683	Camp E.30, Graven Hill, Arncott, Bicester, Oxfordshire
684	Hitcham Park, Hitcham Lane, Burnham, Buckinghamshire
687	Shotover House, Wheatley, Oxfordshire
688	Park camp, West Lulworth, Dorset
693	Durnell's Farm camp (Magazine Camp), Berkshire
693a	Whitchurch camp, Newbury Road, Hampshire, Whitchurch
694	Handy Cross camp, Bideford, Devon
695	Horgard Barracks, Shrivenham, Oxfordshire
1000	Oakhanger camp, Bordon, Hampshire
1001	Crookham Common camp, Thatcham, Berkshire
1003	Capel House camp, Bullsmoor Lane, Enfield, Middlesex
1006	Willems Barracks (West Cavalry Barracks), Hampshire
1009	Northway camp, Ashchurch, Gloucestershire
1011	Camp D.30 Graven Hill, Arncott, Bicester, Oxfordshire
1016	Olddean Common, Camberley, Surrey
1017	No 2 camp, Sheffield Park, Uckfield, Sussex
1020	Shooter's Hill, Woodlands Farm, Woolwich, London
1021	Merley Park camp, Merley, Wimborne Minster, Dorset
1022	Bradninch camp, Bradninch, Exeter, Devon
1025	Histon camp, Milton Road, Cambridge, Cambridgeshire
1026	Raynes Park camp, Bushey Road, Surrey

Scotland

Camp No	Location
2	Woodhouselee camp, Milton Bridge, Midlothian
3	Balhary camp, Perthshire
6	Glenbranter camp, Argyll
12	Donaldson's School, Edinburgh
14	Doonfoot (Bun) camp, Ayrshire
15	Donaldson's School camp, Edinburgh
16	Gosford camp, Longniddry, East Lothian
19	Happenden camp, Douglas, South Lanarkshire
19	Douglas Castle, South Lanarkshire
21	Comrie camp, Perthshire
22	Pennylands camp, Ayrshire
24	Knapedale, Argyll
34	Warebank camp, Orkney
62	The Moor camp, Biggar, Lanarkshire

63	Balhary Estate camp, Perthshire
64	Castle Rankine camp, Denny, Stirlingshire
66	Calvine camp, Blair Atholl, Perthshire
67	Snadyhillock camp, Criagellachie, Banffshire
68	Halmuir Farm camp, Lockerbie, Dumfriesshire
75/76	North Hill camp, Laurencekirk, Kincardineshire
77	Annsmuir camp, Ladybank, Fife
105	Inchdrewer House, Edinburgh
109	Brahan castle, Dingwall, Ross-shire
110	Stuartfield camp, Mintlaw Station, Aberdeenshire
111	Deer Park camp, Monymusk, Aberdeenshire
112	Kingencleugh camp, Mauchline, Ayrshire
113	Holm Park camp, Newton Stewart, Wigtownshire
120	Sunlaws camp, Kelso, Roxburghshire
123	Dalmahey camp, Midlothian
165	Watten camp, Watten, Wick Caithness Base Camp
182	Barony camp, Dumfries Base Camp
188	Johnstone Castle camp, Johnstone, Renfrewshire
230	Stuchendoff (Stuckenduff) camp, Shanden, Helensburgh, Dunbartonshire
236	Nine Wells (Ninewells) camp, Chirnside
242	Cowden camp, Comrie, Perthshire
243	Amisfield camp, Haddington, East Lothian
641	Earls Cross House camp, Dornoch, Sutherland
660	Patterton camp, Thornliebank, Glasgow, Renfrewshire
661	Leffnoll camp, Cairnryan, Stranraer, Wigtownshire
274	Errol Airfield, Errol, Perthshire
275/275a	Kinnell camp, Friockheim, Arbroath, Angus
293	Carronbridge camp, Carronbridge, Dumfries
298	Barony camp, Dumfries
559	Abbeycraig Park, Causeway Head, Stirling
571	ST2, Stranraer, Wigtownshire
582	Blairvadoch camp, Rhu, Helensburgh, Dunbartonshire
612	Honduras camp, Kirkpatrick, Fleming, Dumfriesshire
617	Dryffeholme camp, Lockerbie, Dumfriesshire
640	St Andrew's Hall, St Mary's Isle, Kirkcudbright, Kirkcudbrightshire
1013	Deer Park camp, Dalkeith, Midlothian
1024	Deer Park camp, Dalkeith, Midlothian

Wales

Camp No	Location
11	Island Farm camp, Bridgend, Glamorganshire
29	Claremont, Abergavenny, Monmouthshire
32	Anglesey, Anglesey
38	Pool Park camp, Denbighshire
48	Greenfield Farm, Preisteign, Radnorshire
70	Henllan Bridge camp, Llandyssul, Cardiganshire

101	Glandulas camp, Newtown, Powys
102	Llanddarog camp, Llanddarog, Carmarthenshire
118	Mardy camp, Abergavenny, Monmouthshire
119	Pabo Hall camp, Llandudno Junction, Caernarvonshire
184	Llanmartin camp, Magor, Monmouthshire
197	The Mount, Chepstow, Monmouthshire
198	Island Farm camp, Bridgend, Glamorganshire
199	Ystrad camp, Carmarthen, Carmarthenshire
199	Haverfordwest, Pembrokeshire
200	Llanover Park camp, Llanover, Abergavenny, Monmouthshire
234	Talgarth Hospital, Talgarth, Breconshire
252	Abergwili Hospital, Abergwili, Carmarthen, Carmarthenshire
284	Abbey Road camp, Neath, Glamorganshire
284	Swanbridge, Sully, Glamorganshire
408	Penclawdd, Swansea, Glamorganshire
573	Pendre camp, Builth Wells, Radnorshire
677	New Inn camp, Pontypool, Monmouthshire
697	Royal Artillery Practice camp, Sennybridge, Breconshire
1014	Ordnance Storage Depot (OSD), Flintshire

Ireland

Camp No	Location
5	Monrush camp, County Tyrone
10	Gosford camp, County Armagh
11	Gillford, County Armagh
12	Elmfield camp, County Armagh
14	Holywood, Belfast
161	Belfast Military Hospital, Belfast County Down
172	Holywood camp, Belfast County Down Base Camp
173	Rockport, Belfast County Down Base Camp
187	Dungannon, County Tyrone
190	Lisanoure camp, Loughgiel, Cloughmills, County Antrim
190	Cloughmills, County Tyrone
682	Rockport, Craigavan, County Down
682	Holywood camp, Belfast, County Down

Isle of Man and Channel Islands

Camp No	Location
171	Isle of Man camp, Mereside Empire Terrace, Douglas, Isle of Man
702	Jurby, Isle of Man
801	Castel camp, Guernsey, Channel Islands Base Camp
802	Fort Regent, Jersey, Channel Islands Base Camp

BIBLIOGRAPHY

Few books have been written on the subject of prisoners held in Britain during the war. As such, most of the material in this book has been taken from original documents. However, the following volumes were consulted:

Brown, R. Douglas, *East Anglia 1943*, Hyperion Books, 1990.
———, *East Anglia 1944*, Hyperion Books, 1990.
Faulk, Henry, *Group Captives*, Chatto and Windus, 1977.
Moltmann, Jurgen, *A Broad Place: An Autobiography*, SCM Press, 2007.
Scotland, Lt Col Alexander P., *The London Cage*, Evans Brothers Limited, 1957.

INDEX